# The
# BIG BOOK
# OF JUICING

The

# BIG BOOK OF JUICING

## 150 of the Best Recipes for Fruit and Vegetable Juices, Green Smoothies, and Probiotic Drinks

Skyhorse Publishing

Skyhorse Publishing books may be purchased in bulk at special discounts for sales promotion, corporate gifts, fund-raising, or educational purposes. Special editions can also be created to specifications. For details, contact the Special Sales Department, Skyhorse Publishing, 307 West 36th Street, 11th Floor, New York, NY 10018 or info@ skyhorsepublishing.com.

Skyhorse® and Skyhorse Publishing® are registered trademarks of Skyhorse Publishing, Inc.®, a Delaware corporation.

Visit our website at www.skyhorsepublishing.com.

10 9 8 7 6 5 4 3 2 1

Library of Congress Cataloging-in-Publication Data is available on file.

Print ISBN: 978-1-63450-487-4
Ebook ISBN: 978-1-5107-0160-1

Printed in China

## Materials in this book are pulled from the following sources:

**Delicious Probiotic Drinks** by Julia Mueller
www.theroastedroot.net

**Detox Juicing** by Morena Cuadra and Morena Escardó
www.wellnessforeveryone.com

**Green Smoothie Joy** by Cressida Elias

**Green Smoothies and Protein Drinks** by Jason Manheim
www.healthygreendrink.com

**The Green Smoothie Miracle** by Erica Palmcrantz, photography by Anna Hult
www.rawfoodbyerica.se

**The Complete Juicer** by Abigail R. Gehring

**The Healthy Green Drink Diet** by Jason Manheim
www.healthygreendrink.com

**The Healthy Juicer's Bible** by Farnoosh Brock
www.prolificjuicing.com

**The Healthy Probiotic Diet** by R.J. Ruppenthal

Available through Skyhorse Publishing, www.skyhorsepublishing.com, and wherever books are sold.

# Contents

# PART I:
# ALL ABOUT JUICING

# The Benefits of Juicing

If you're buying this book, you're probably already enough of a juicing fan to know that drinking fresh-squeezed juice makes you feel great. But in case you're looking for ways to convince your friends and family to join the juicing revolution, here are some specific reasons:

- **Weight Loss:** Oftentimes we feel hungry not because we need more calories but because our bodies are craving more nutrients. One glass of juice can provide you with several servings of nutrient-rich fruits and vegetables, and it's easier for your body to absorb nutrients from juice than it is from whole produce. When you drink fresh, raw juice, you may find that you don't need to eat nearly as often or as much.

- **Digestive Health:** There's no doubt that digestive problems are on the rise, especially in America. Sometimes it seems like everyone I know has some sort of digestive disorder, whether it be Crohn's, collitis, ulcers, persistent heartburn, irritable bowl syndrome (IBS), or undiagnosed nausea, bloating, or abdominal pains. While these conditions can be caused by a range of issues, they have the common outcome that when you're suffering with any of them, it's tough to get the nutrition your body needs to be healthy and whole. Juicing gives your digestive system a rest so that it can begin to heal.

The vitamins, minerals, and enzymes packed in the juice are absorbed into your bloodstream quickly, without taxing your digestive organs in the same way that the fibers in whole raw produce do.

- **Increased Energy and Mental Clarity:** When your digestive system has less work to do, you have more energy for other things, including thinking. Everyone knows that after eating a heavy meal you're likely to feel like taking a long nap. It takes a lot of energy to digest all that food, leaving little left over for anything else. Not only is a glass of juice less work for your body to process, but the intense concentration of nutrients will leave you feeling revitalized and mentally sharp.

- **Taste:** Okay, not all vegetable juices are created equal when it comes to flavor. You may have had a green juice from a juice stand that made you want to gag. But healthy juices can also be really delicious! Add some lemon and fresh ginger to any green juice to brighten up the flavor, or throw in an apple, pear, or a handful of grapes for more sweetness. Some vegetables, such as beets and carrots, are naturally sweet and are great for getting kids to appreciate vegetable juices.

# Choosing a Juicer

There are two main types of automatic juicers (as opposed to manual juicers, which are mainly for hand squeezing citrus fruits): masticating juicers and centrifugal juicers. If you do a quick search online, the first thing you'll notice is that masticating juicers are much more expensive, starting at around $200, whereas you can get a good quality centrifugal juicer for about $100. So what's the difference, other than price?

**Centrifugal juicers** have an upright design and function by spinning really fast while the produce is chewed up, causing the juice to spin to the edges of the container and drain into your cup while the pulp is caught in the bowl of the machine. Centrifugal juicers are easy to use, work quickly, and are just fine for most fruits and non-leafy vegetables. You can certainly juice your leafy greens in a centrifugal (I do all the time), but you'll get less juice and more pulp than you would with a masticating juicer. One tip is to wrap your greens around a dense vegetable, such as a carrot—this will help feed the greens through the chute. Also, wheatgrass tends to clog up centrifugal juicers, so if you're a big fan of the grass, you'll want to invest in a masticating juicer or a juicer specifically made for wheatgrass.

**Masticating juicers** do just what they sound like they should—they chew up your produce by crushing it and squeezing it against the walls of the juicer. They then separate the juice from the pulp, generally leaving you with more juice and less pulp than a centrifugal juicer would. Masticating juicers do a great job juicing leafy greens. On the other hand, you have to chop up large produce into small pieces, since they tend to have smaller chutes, which requires a bit of extra time. There is some concern that a centrifugal juicer heats the produce up enough that some of the enzymes are destroyed, leaving you with less nutritious juice. However, produce has to be heated to 118°F in order to lose its nutrition, which is unlikely to happen, especially if you start with cold produce. But if you're concerned about this, a masticating juicer does spin at a much slower speed and so will create less friction, and, thus, heat your produce less.

In short, here's my juicer advice: If you want a juicer that works quickly and requires minimal prep time and less initial investment, get yourself a centrifugal juicer for around $100–$150. If you plan to juice a lot of sprouts and/or wheatgrass, are willing to take a few more minutes on prep time, and have the money to put down now, get a masticating juicer in the $200–$300 range (you may end up saving money in the long run, as you'll get more juice from your produce). If an upfront investment is of no concern, a masticating juicer in the $500–$600 range will suck even more juice out of your produce and yield highly nutritious juice.

I recommend browsing online and reading various juicer reviews before making a purchase. Not all brands are created equal, but you also don't need to spend a fortune to get a perfectly good juicer.

# Choosing Produce

Growing your own produce is the healthiest and most economical way to get your juicing ingredients. But unless you live in a climate that's warm year-round, chances are you won't be growing everything you want to include in your juice all the time. When shopping for produce, think about the following:

1. **Choose organic.** I know it's usually more expensive, and it's true that you can make perfectly tasty juice from non-organic produce, but you're probably juicing largely for the health benefits, and there's no question that organic produce is healthier. Even if you wash your fruits and vegetables thoroughly, they will have absorbed some of the pesticides and herbicides used on the fields they were grown in, and for all kinds of reasons you don't want to put that stuff in your body. Also, produce that is not grown organically will often contain smaller amounts of the vitamins and minerals your body needs. If your budget won't allow all organic produce, at least choose organic for the following, whenever possible: apples, bell peppers, blueberries, celery, cherry tomatoes, collard greens, cucumbers, grapes, hot peppers, kale, lettuce, zucchini, nectarines, and peaches. These are at the highest risk for pesticide residue.

2. **Choose fresh.** Avoid produce that is wilted, slimy, limp, overly soft, or turning brown. Some fruits and vegetables last longer than others. Dense produce can be bought in greater bulk, since it will last longer: this includes apples, carrots, and sweet potatoes. Of the greens, kale tends to last the longest.

3. **Choose variety.** My grandmother's favorite maxim was "everything in moderation." If you drink a whole head of cabbage every morning, your body's not going to be thrilled with you. Mix and match your fruits and veggies so that you're getting a wide range of nutrients and not overloading your system with any one thing.

# What NOT to Juice

There are some things that really aren't worth juicing, either because they're very bitter, they don't contain enough juice to make it worthwhile, or they'll damage your juicer. Many of these fruits and veggies are great for blending, but would be a waste to try to juice. Also only juice fresh produce—again, you can blend frozen or thawed produce, but don't juice. And don't juice any plant part that you're not absolutely sure is edible. There are many types of leaves, stems, or roots that should not be consumed. Here's a list of the most common things you might think you can juice but shouldn't:

Rinds. With the exception of lemon and lime rinds, avoid putting rinds through your juicer.

Avocado

Banana

Carrot greens (not edible!)

Coconut (you can add coconut water to your juices, but don't put the meat through your juicer)

Edamame

Eggplant

Green beans

Mustard greens

Okra

Onions or leeks

Papaya peels

Potatoes (other than sweet potatoes)

Squashes

Wild parsnips (cultivated ones are fine)

# A Few Cautions

Juicing isn't rocket science and you shouldn't be intimidated by the process. But there are a few cautions to keep in mind.

- Juicing shouldn't replace eating for long periods of time. Sticking to juice for a few days to detox your body is fine, but juicing removes most of the fiber in your produce, and eventually your body is going to crave that. You can also mix back in some of the pulp to add fiber to your juice.

- Not all juices are low calorie. If you're trying to lose weight, avoid or limit produce with the highest sugar content. These include tangerines, cherries, grapes, pomegranates, mangos, figs, and bananas for the fruits. High-sugar veggies include beets, carrots, corn, parsnips, peas, plantains, and sweet potatoes.

- It's best to drink your juice right away. It loses nutrients as it sits, but it will also go bad after a while, even if covered and refrigerated.

- If you have health issues or are on any medications, it's a good idea to discuss juicing with your doctor. Kale, for example, contains a high concentration of Vitamin K, which promotes blood clotting and can counteract blood thinners. Raw kale can also suppress thyroid function in certain people.

# What About All That Pulp?

When you see all that pulp piling up in your juicer, you're going to feel wasteful. Unless you use it for something! Here are some ideas:

- Compost it!

- If you have chickens, they'll eat it.

- Mix it into pasta dishes, salads, or into cream cheese or sour cream for a delicious and nutritious dip.

- Add it to soups, stews, and broth.

- Add it to breads, muffins, cookies, or pancakes. It's not that weird, really. Think about zucchini bread—same idea.

- Make crackers!

# Tips for a Juicing Detox

A short detox can be a great way to jumpstart weight loss, clear your body of toxins, give your digestive system a break, and get you going on a healthier diet. Here are some tips for your juicing detox.

- Plan to detox for 1–3 days. Generally speaking, juice is not meant to replace food for longer than that. Longer detoxes can be helpful in certain situations. If you feel your body needs a 5- or 7-day detox, talk to a doctor and do your own research before you begin.

- For 3 days before your detox, start limiting or cutting out completely certain foods and beverages, such as coffee, tea, soda, sugar, meat, dairy, alcohol, and wheat. Easing off these things gradually make your detox easier and may make it more effective.

- During the detox, plan to consume 32 to 96 ounces of juice a day, making sure your juices are at least 50 percent from vegetables.

- Drink plenty of water during the detox to clear out your system between juices.

- Drink your juices slowly and plan to have one every two hours. This will help to keep your blood sugar even, which helps prevent dizziness, mood swings, and cravings.

- If you need to make your juice for the whole day all at once, store the juice you're not going to drink immediately in a glass jar with a tight lid, and keep it refrigerated until you drink it.

- Don't plan to be very physically active during your fast. Your body will be processing plenty without the additional strain.

- After the detox, reintroduce food gradually over several days.

# Healing Chart

If you have a particular condition, use this chart to customize juices to meet your needs.

| Condition | Beneficial Juice Ingredients |
|---|---|
| Arthritis | Blueberries, Broccoli, Cantaloupe, Carrots, Cherries, Grapes, Grapefruits, Kale, Kiwi, Spinach, Strawberries, Papaya, Pineapple, Tangerines, Oranges, Apricots |
| Cancer | Apples, Apricots, Beets, Broccoli, Brussels Sprouts, Cabbage, Garlic, Kale, Kiwi, Oranges, Pears, Spinach, Strawberries, Wheatgrass |
| Diabetes | Asparagus, Blueberries, Broccoli, Celery, Cranberries, Raspberries, Spinach, Tomatoes |
| Digestive Problems | Apples, Blueberries, Cabbage, Carrots, Celery, Mint, Papaya, Parsley, Pineapple |
| Exhaustion | Apples, Carrots, Ginger, Grapefruits, Lemons, Mint, Oranges, Tangerines |
| Overweight | Apples, Arugula, Broccoli, Brussels Sprouts, Cabbage, Cauliflower, Ginger, Kale, Lemon, Radishes, Turnips, Watercress |
| Skin Problems | Apricots, Beets, Broccoli, Cabbage, Carrots, Cucumbers, Lettuce, Sprouts, Sweet Potatoes |

# Produce Nutrition Guide

# Apples

Apples are full of antioxidants, which boost your immune system and help fight a wide range of diseases. In some studies, apple juice was shown to improve brain function and decrease the risk of Alzheimer's. The phytonutrients in apples also help to regulate your blood sugar. Apple juice has anti-inflammatory and anti-viral properties and helps to detoxify the digestive track.

To juice, cut in halves or quarters and push slowly through the juicer, peels and all. The seeds don't need to be removed as they'll be caught with the pulp.

# Beets and Beet Greens

Beet roots (the red part you normally think of when you think of beets) contain calcium, sulfur, iron, potassium, choline, beta-carotene, and Vitamin C. They are also very high in minerals that strengthen the liver and gall bladder and act as the building blocks for blood corpuscles and cells. Just 22 calories of beet greens contain 14 percent of our daily recommended dose of iron, 127 percent of Vitamin A, 50 percent of Vitamin C, and more calcium per calorie than milk. Beets also contain phytochemicals and antioxidants that may help to fight and prevent cancer.

To juice, wash the beet roots well with your hands, removing all dirt, and rinse off the leaves. Juice the roots, stem, and leaves until a stream of brightly colored juice pours out. When using a centrifugal juicer, alternate between beets and carrots to prevent the beet pulp from building up. When using a masticating juicer, alternate between beets and apples to prevent clogs.

# Blueberries

Blueberries are a good source of colon-cleansing pectin, Vitamin C, K, manganese, and potassium. Plus, blueberries are a fantastic source of antioxidants and anti-inflammatories. Where most fruits have between three and five different kinds of anthocyanin pigments, blueberries have been found to contain as many as twenty-five or thirty. This abundance makes blueberries one of the best foods for protecting our brains as we age, which also means that blueberries may protect from the onset of Alzheimer's disease.

Juicing blueberries is easy. Just rinse them off and pop them into your juicer. The bouncy little berries have a tendency to try and jump back out again, so make sure to quickly insert your tamper after pouring in the berries. Additionally, try to drink anything made with blueberries within an hour of juicing, as the amount of pectin in blueberries will soon turn any juice made with them into a thick, unappetizing goo.

# Broccoli

Broccoli is a fantastic vegetable that has tons of healthy vitamins and minerals. Broccoli is high in Vitamin C, Vitamin A, and also contains iron and calcium. It's also high in protein, Vitamin B1, sulfur, and potassium. Lastly, broccoli is very high in phytochemicals and antioxidants, especially sulforaphane and indoles. Both of these compounds help to cleanse the body of carcinogens and may help to fight cancer.

To juice broccoli, simply wash and cut to fit into the hopper. Alternate with apple to keep everything running smoothly and to reduce strain on your juicer's motor.

# Brussels Sprouts

Brussels sprouts may be small, but they're packed with a ton of nutritious vitamins and minerals. One cup of Brussels sprouts contains only 58 calories, but has 162 percent of your daily recommended dose of Vitamin C and 10 percent of iron. They are also a great source of manganese, potassium, folate, thiamin, riboflavin, and Vitamins B6, A, and K. They also have an impressive amount of phytochemicals, which help to fight cancer.

Juice Brussels sprouts by rinsing them off and dumping them into the juicer.

# Carrots

Carrot juice causes the liver to release bile and excess accumulated cholesterol. It also has an alkalizing effect on the blood, soothing the entire nervous system and toning intestinal walls. Carrots help to prevent kidney stones by acting as a detoxifier for the liver and digestive track. Plus, despite one medium carrot having only 30 calories, it contains 330 percent of your daily requirement of Vitamin A. Carrots are also rich in organic calcium, Vitamin C, most of the B vitamins, plus iron, potassium phosphorus, and sodium. The Vitamin A in carrots also acts as an antioxidant that binds to free radicals, which are associated with cancer growth.

To juice your carrots, cut off the tops and the tips and stick them in your juicer. To lighten the flavor of carrot juice, add a half or whole lemon when juicing.

# Celery

Celery juice is a very good cource of Vitamin C, folic acid, potassium, and Vitamins B1 and B6. It also has a lot of sodium which, combined with the potassium, make for a great post workout drink. It works to replace electrolytes and offsets muscle cramps and fatigue. In addition to all this, celery juice has a good collection of phytochemicals that helps fight cancer, lower blood pressure, improve the vascular system, and decrease the suffering of migraines.

To juice, simply break off, rinse, and juice the whole stalk, leaves and all. If using a centrifugal juicer, juice the celery last because it is very stringy and can clog the side of the basket.

# Cherries

Cherries are a good source of Vitamin C. They also contain two powerful phytochemicals, quercetin and anthcyanidins. These can both help to reduce the risk of asthma and lung cancer. Anthcyanidins also reduce inflammation as effectively as aspirin and ibuprofen. Finally, cherries contain a good amount of melatonin, otherwise known as the body's bedtime drug. Melatonin can aid insomnia and may help to alleviate depression.

To juice cherries, you must first remove the pits, as time-consuming as that is.

# Cucumbers

Cucumber juice is full of Vitamins A, C, and K, as well as phosphorus, pantothenic acid, manganese, magnesium, and potassium. Cucumbers also contain silicon, a mineral that the body uses to improve skin, nails, and hair. Silicon also helps combat insomnia and tuberculosis.

Juice the cucumber with the skin on, as many nutrients are found just under the skin. Cucumbers have a high water content, and so produce a lot of juice.

# Ginger

Ginger is a good source of Vitamin C, copper, manganese, and potassium, but it is perhaps most well known for its effectiveness in reducing the symptoms of gastrointestinal disorders. It is also quite popular as a remedy for motion sickness, especially for sea sickness, and, for many people, is more effective in this regard than Dramamine. Ginger also absorbs gastrointestinal toxins, hormones, and stomach acids, making it an effective treatment for the nausea and vomiting associated with pregnancy. Ginger also contains powerful antioxidants called gingerals that inhibit the formation of inflammatory compounds in the body and also have direct anti-inflammatory effects.

To juice ginger, simply wash it and put it in your juicer, skin and all. Always juice ginger first so that the other produce can capture any remaining healing volatile oils still in the machine.

# Grapes

Grapes are a great source of Vitamin K, manganese, and potassium. Grapes have become known for cleansing the liver and removing uric acid from the body. Red grape juice, especially from Concord grapes, has flavonoids that can prevent the oxidation of bad cholesterol that leads to buildup of plaque in artery walls. The flavonoids in red grape juice also keep the arteries elastic, which helps to prevent atherosclerosis.

To juice grapes, wash them well and drop them into the juicer. You can juice them stems and all. It can be useful to scrape the skins out of the basket a few times during juicing, as the screen becomes clogged and the yield will be reduced.

# Grapefruit

One cup of chopped grapefruit contains 120 percent of your daily recommended dose of Vitamin C and 53 percent of Vitamin A. Grapefruit is also a good source of potassium, thiamin, folte, and magnesium. In addition to all of this, grapefruits contain an array of antioxidant-regenerating phytochemicals, including limonene, limonin, nomolin, and naringenin. All of these phytochemicals may help to prevent lung and colon cancer.

To juice, cut the outer yellow peel with a sharp knife, leaving as much of the white pith as possible. After removing the peel, simply stick the flesh of the fruit in your juicer. No need to remove the seeds before juicing.

# Kale

Kale is definitely king of the superfoods. It is a rich source of Vitamin K, beta-carotene, Vitamin C, lutein, zeaxanthin, and an excellent source of calcium. Only 50 calories of kale contains 200 percent of your daily requirement of Vitamin C, 308 percent of Vitamin A, and 15 percent of calcium. Kale is also a good source of iron, folate, thiamin, riboflavin, magnesium, phosphorus, potassium, copper, and manganese. All the nutrients make kale an anti-inflammatory food, a cancer fighter, an anti-depressant in some cases, and good for skin and weight loss.

The Vitamin K in kale helps blood to clot, so if you are taking blood thinners, discuss with your doctor before including it in your juices. Kale also contains oxalates, which have been associated with kidney stones and gallstones. Finally, in some people, kale suppresses thyroid function. If you are concerned, speak with your doctor or naturopath. It may be wise to forego kale juice or limit consumption to a couple of times a week.

Kale is a little tough to juice, owing to the toughness of its leaves. To make the process run a little smoother, push the kale through with a wedge of apple or a carrot, a little at a time, throughout the juicing process.

# Lemons

Lemons are very high in Vitamin C. Just one cup of lemon juice contains 187 percent of your daily required dose of Vitamin C and is also a good source of folate and potassium. Lemons are great for detoxifying the body. During juice fasts, lemon juice has a fantastic ability to dissolve mucus and scour toxins from the cellular tissue. Lemons are also a diuretic and contain the phytochemical limonene, which has been shown to be effective in dissolving gallstones and protecting against all kinds of cancers.

When juicing lemons, be sure to leave some of the white inner peel to get the bioflavonoid, limonene. No need to remove the seeds prior to juicing.

## Lettuce

Fourteen calories (85 grams) of Romaine lettuce will provide 148 percent of the daily recommended dose of Vitamin A, 34 percent of Vitamin C, and 5 percent of iron. Lettuce is also a good source of Vitamin K, thiamin, folate, potassium, manganese, riboflavin, calcium, Vitamin B6, copper, and magnesium. Romaine lettuce contains cancer fighting carotenoids. Plus the mix of sulfur, chlorine, silicon, and B complex vitamins contribute to healthy skin and defend against lung cancer.

To juice lettuce, simply rinse the leaves and put them in the juicer. Push the leaves through with a carrot.

# Mint

Mint soothes stomach indigestion and inflammation and can reduce nausea and motion sickness. It can also help reduce congestion in the nose, throat, bronchi, and lungs. In addition, it's a natural stimulant. Recent research shows that certain enzymes in mint may help prevent and treat cancer.

# Oranges

A single cup of orange juice has 207 percent of your daily recommended dose of Vitamin C. Oranges are also a great source of thiamin, folate, and potassium. Plus they have lots of disease fighting antioxidants that rid the body of free radicals. On top of all this, orange juice boosts your immune system, increases iron absorption, reduces inflammation, lowers hypertension, and increases good cholesterol while lowering bad cholesterol.

To juice oranges, cut the peel off with a sharp knife. Keep as much as possible of the white pith underneath the peel, as it's particularly full of nutrients.

# Parsley

Parsley is a humble herb best known for garnishing fancy dishes. But this unassuming sprig is so much more. One cup, containing only 22 calories, has 133 percent of our daily recommended dose of Vitamin C, 101 percent of Vitamin A, and 21 percent of iron. Parsley is also a great source of fiber, Vitamin K, calcium, magnesium, potassium, copper, and magnesium. It's a good source of protein, Vitamin E, thiamin, riboflavin, niacin, Vitamin B6, zinc, phosphorous, and pantothenic acid. Parsley is also one of the best sources of chlorophyll, which acts like iron to oxidize the blood. It's also a great veggie to detox with as it cleanses the kidneys, liver, and urinary tract.

Juicing parsley is as easy as rinsing and popping it into your juicer. To maximize the yield, push the parsley through with an apple or a carrot.

## Pears

Pears are a great source of pectin and fiber, not to mention a good source of Vitamins C, B2, and E, plus copper and potassium. Pears are actually higher in pectin, which acts as a diuretic and a mild laxative, than apples. On top of all this, pears may lower your risk of developing asthma and contain hydroxycinnamic acid, which helps to prevent stomach cancer.

To juice pears, just wash them and then put them in the juicer, skin, stems, seeds, and all.

# Spinach

Spinach, made famous by Popeye, is high in Vitamins A, C, and E. It is also a good source of choline, calcium, potassium, iron, and folic acid. One cup of juiced spinach has 10 grams of protein and spinach has 14 times the iron per calorie than red meat. Spinach is also one of the highest sources of lutein, which protects your eyes from macular degeneration (a condition that causes blindness in old age), and fights cancer. Spinach also has a lot of glutathione and alpha lipoic acid. Glutathione is an antioxidant that protects DNA from oxidation, detoxifies pollutants and carcinogens, boosts the immune system, aids healthy cellular reproduction, and reduces chronic inflammation. Alpha lipoic acid is both water and fat soluble, meaning that it can defend every kind of cell from oxidative assaults.

Most spinach that you buy comes prewashed and can be juiced as is. If you have loose spinach or are growing your own, just rinse the leaves off well and juice.

# Strawberries

Strawberries are very high in Vitamin C; just one cup contains 149 percent of our daily recommended dose. Strawberries are also a good source of folate, manganese, potassium, sodium, and iron. Plus one-and-a-half cups of strawberries contain 3,500 ORAC units, or Oxygen Radical Absorbance Capacity units. ORACs protect us against oxidative stress. Strawberries also protect against the damage caused by free radicals and contain phenolic acids that may prevent esophageal and colon tumors and encourage cell death in cancer cells.

Juicing strawberries is easy. Just rinse them off and juice them, stems and all.

# PART II: SMOOTHIES

# Why, What, How, When, Where Green Smoothies?

## Why Drink Green Smoothies?

- Green smoothies give your digestive system a break from ordinary food, which leads to increased energy.
- You automatically and significantly reduce your oil and salt intake.
- When you drink two to three cups (500–750 ml) of green smoothies daily, you get enough greens to nourish your body, and all of the beneficial nutrients are well absorbed.
- The chlorophyll boosts your cells and you shine more.
- It's an investment in your health.
- You might lose some unnecessary extra pounds and reach your natural weight.
- Your eyes begin to sparkle.
- You oxygenate the body and provide it with calcium, chlorophyll, liquid, and vitality through biophotons and live enzymes.

## What is a Green Smoothie?

- A nutritious drink that's composed of green leaves, fruit, and water. The proportions of the drink are optimal for humans, as 60 percent of the drink consists of organic, ripe fruit and 40 percent of green leaves.

- A drink "invented" by Victoria Boutenko.
- Similar to what the chimpanzees eat and "thrive on."

## How to Make a Green Smoothie?

What you need:
- Green leaves, fruit, water.
- A cutting board and a knife.
- A colander or a salad spinner for rinsing your green leaves.
- A glass, bottle, or thermos, if you want your smoothie to go.
- A blender. There are many different kinds of blenders, and they range widely in price and strength. Once you get started with your smoothies, it's worth investing in a blender that's a little more expensive. It will be quicker and stronger, and it will allow you to crush frozen fruit and berries, which are included in the delicious green ice cream smoothies.

## When to Have Green Smoothies?

- Breakfast—for the best start to your day. If you travel to work by car, bus, or subway, it's easy to bring your smoothie with you.
- Snack—instead of a coffee, refuel with the real and easy energy of a smoothie.
- Lunch—a quick lunch that's easy to carry.
- Before and after exercise—the perfect workout meal. Feel free to boost your smoothie with rice or hemp protein powder after a workout.

- Dinner—feels good for the body and enables it to rest overnight. The smoothie doesn't burden the system as much as a "regular" dinner, so it's fine to drink it a little later at night. If you work nights, it's the perfect way for the body to get digestible nutrients and food that passes through the body quickly.

It's not about replacing all your meals with a green smoothie. A friend of mine started to replace her morning sandwich with a smoothie. The rest of the day she ate as she normally would. If you eat five meals a day, this means it's a 25 percent improvement in your overall diet. If you want to undergo a cleanse, you can replace all your meals with a green smoothie.

## Where to Have a Green Smoothie?

- A green soup is the perfect appetizer or a light dinner.
- At a picnic.
- With friends.
- While you're waiting for the subway.
- You can drink a smoothie at anywhere and at any time!

# Grandma Love

Collards such as kale flourish in the winter and provide a great green alternative.

This is one of my green winter favorites.

2 cups green kale
2 cups water
1 apple
1 pear
3 dates
1 tbsp lúcuma

*Blend the minced green kale with water. Add pieces of the apple and pear and pitted dates and blend again. Add one tbsp of lúcuma and mix. Add more water until desired consistency is reached.*

# Asian Green Smoothie

Bok choy is common in the Asian kitchen. Usually steamed or stir-fried, it's also ideal as a green base in a smoothie!

1 cup bok choy
1 cup green beans
1 cup alfalfa sprouts
½–1 tbsp fresh ginger, peeled
2 cups water
1 tbsp lime juice
2 pears

*Blend the bok choy and pieces of green beans, alfalfa sprouts, and small pieces of peeled ginger with the water. Add lime and pieces of pear. Blend again. Add water until desired consistency is reached.*

# Refresh

Grapefruit provides a tangy, slightly bitter taste, which makes for a fresh-tasting smoothie.

**2 handfuls of kale**
**1½ cups water**
**1 grapefruit, peeled and separated into segments**
**½ avocado**

*Chop up the kale and mix with water. Add the grapefruit segments and scooped-out avocado and blend again.*

# Sprout Smoothie

Sprouts contain lots of nutrients and living enzymes, including chlorophyll.

Add them to the other greens to optimize your smoothie.

**2 cups spinach**
**1 cup green lentil sprouts**
**2 cups water**
**1 large pear**
**1 tbsp açaí**
**½ tbsp of camu camu**
**1 avocado**

*Blend spinach and green lentil sprouts with water. Add the chopped pears, açaí, camu camu and mix again. Add the scooped-out avocado. Dilute with water until desired consistency is reached.*

# Apple Glory

Eating apples every day builds a great foundation for good health. An apple a day keeps the doctor away!

2 apples
2 cups spinach
2 cups water
½ avocado

*Chop the apple into pieces and blend it with spinach and water. Mix again. Add water until desired consistency is reached.*

# Cacao Dessert Smoothie

A smoothie that's lunch and dessert in one!

2 handfuls of kale
2 cups of water
2 dates
2 tbsps raw cacao powder
1 tbsp honey
1 avocado

*Chop the kale and mix with the water. Add the pitted dates, cacao, and honey and blend again. Add scooped-out avocado and more water until desired consistency is reached.*

# Green Pear Smoothie

Use ripe pears for a smoother and creamier smoothie.

2 large handfuls of kale
2 cups water
2 large pears, ripe
1 cup blueberries, frozen

*Blend chopped kale with the water. Add pieces of pears and blueberries and mix again. Dilute with water for desired consistency.*

# Daily Green Smoothie

Many of the green smoothies are based on what you have at home. Here is a variation on my "I'll use what I have" smoothie!

2 cups mixed salad
2 cups water
½ cup broccoli
½ inch cucumber
1 kiwi
2 pears
½ avocado

*Mix the salad with the water. Add pieces of broccoli and cucumber.*

*Blend. Add pieces of kiwi and pears. Scoop out the avocado and mix into the smoothie. Add more water until desired consistency is reached.*

# Garden Smoothie

Wild leaves are really the best green leaves that you can use in your smoothie. Miner's lettuce is one of my favorites, and it grows right outside my house. Organic, locally grown, and free!

2 cups miner's lettuce (or other wild green leaves)
1 tbsp hemp protein powder

1–2 cups water
2 cups honeydew melon

*Mix miner's lettuce with hemp seed protein powder and water. Cut honeydew melon into pieces and add to mixture. Add more water until desired consistency is reached.*

# Fresh!

Serve with ice cubes for a really fresh and delicious smoothie. Mint is also good for digestion.

1 cup mint
1–2 cups water
2 pears
1 tbsp lime juice

*Blend chopped mint with one cup of water. Add cut-up pears and lime juice, and mix again. Dilute with more water until desired consistency is reached.*

# Strawberrylicious

Fresh and cool strawberry smoothie! Basil and strawberries are both rich in iron.

2 cups strawberries
2 cups basil
1 tbsp lime juice

1 cup water
½ cup ice cubes
Optional; honey to sweeten

*Mix strawberries, basil, lime juice, and water. Add ice cubes and mix again.*

# Green Lúcuma Smoothie

Lúcuma is a superfood that contains high levels of B3 and iron and gives the smoothie a creamy, caramel flavor.

1½ cups lettuce
2 cups water
1 pear
1 apple
1 small zucchini
2 tbsps lúcuma

*Chop the lettuce and mix with water. Cut the pear, apple, and zucchini into pieces and add. Blend again. Add the lúcuma and dilute with water until desired consistency is reached.*

# Green Smoothie with Chaga Tea

Chaga grows on trees and is super-nutritious and especially rich in antioxidants. It's the perfect base for a green smoothie.

2 cups spinach
2 cups chaga tea
2 celery stalks
½ cucumber
1 apple

⅛ inch ginger, peeled
1 avocado

*Blend spinach with chaga tea. Cut celery, cucumber, ginger, and apple into pieces. Add the ingredients to the blender and mix. Scoop out the avocado and add more water until desired consistency is reached.*

# Sea-buckthorn Smoothie

Sea-buckthorn can be purchased fresh or frozen. It's rich in Vitamin C and antioxidants, which make your skin glow.

1 cup lettuce
1 cup sunflower shoots
1 cup sea-buckthorn
2 cups water

*Mix all the ingredients with water. Add more water until desired consistency is reached.*

# Green Orange

Spruce up your traditional orange juice with spinach. Kids love it!

2 cups orange juice
2 cups spinach

*Blend the ingredients and enjoy!*

# Iron Smoothie

Parsley contains lots of iron, which is especially good for women.

2 cups flat-leaf parsley
2 cups water
2 apples
1 zucchini
1 tbsp lemon juice

*Mix parsley with water. Cut apples and zucchini into pieces. Add remaining ingredients and blend again. Dilute with more water until desired consistency is reached.*

# Green Kiwi Smoothie

Kiwi is a fruit that isn't too sweet and gives the smoothie a tart, fresh taste reminiscent of yogurt.

**6 inch cucumber**
**1 kiwi**
**2 cups lettuce**
**1 tbsp lemon juice**
**1 avocado**
**1 tbsp lemon juice**
**1–2 cups of water**

*Cut the cucumber and kiwi into chunks. Mix together with lettuce, scooped-out avocado, lemon juice, and water. Dilute with water until desired consistency is reached.*

# Apricot & Melon Smoothie

This is a real summer smoothie with melon and fresh orange apricots. It's spiked with the power of sunflower shoots and spinach, and it's also hydrating because of the cucumber and water. Bring it in a thermos to the beach!

**2 cups melon**
**4 inches cucumber**
**1 cup apricot**
**1 cup spinach**
**1 cup sunflower shoots**
**2 cups water**

*Cut the melon, cucumber, and apricots into chunks. Mix with spinach, sunflower shoots, and water. Dilute with water until desired consistency is reached.*

# Green Passion

Passion fruit gives this smoothie a tart flavor, and the creaminess derives from the banana . . . Exotic!

1 cup spinach
2 cups water
3 passion fruits
2 bananas

*Blend the spinach with water. Scoop out the pulp from the passion fruit and add together with peeled and sliced bananas. Mix. Add more water until desired consistency is reached.*

# Green Broccoli Smoothie

Broccoli contains more starch than green leaves, which makes for a more filling smoothie!

1 cup broccoli
2 pears
1 cup spinach
1 cup sunflower shoots
3 tbsps lemon juice
3 cups water

*Cut the broccoli and pear into pieces. Mix with spinach, sunflower shoots, lemon juice and water. Dilute with more water until desired consistency is reached.*

# Apple Green

Arugula has a spicy taste and adds a peppery flavor to the smoothie.

The bitterness of the arugula promotes digestion.

**2 handfuls of arugula**
**1–2 cups water**
**2 apples, red**
**½ inch cucumber**
**1 tsp lemon juice**
**½ avocado**

*Blend arugula with 1 cup of water. Cut the apple and cucumber into pieces. Add the remaining ingredients, except for the avocado, and blend again. Add the scooped-out avocado and mix, dilute with water until desired consistency is reached.*

# Pomegreen Smoothie

Tip! To pick out the small red pomegranate seeds, cut the fruit in half, gently squeeze the skin, and turn it inside out over a bowl. Remove the seeds. Discard the white parts of the skin, which can taste bitter. Strain the juice, pour into a beautiful glass, and add the kernels to the smoothie.

**2 cups salad**
**1–2 cups water**
**2 pears**
**1 cup (about ½ pomegranate)**
**  pomegranate kernels**

*Blend the salad with 1 cup of water. Cut the pear into pieces and add the other ingredients before mixing again. Add more water until desired consistency is reached.*

# Green Grape Smoothie

Whenever you buy grapes, you should look for organic ones with seeds.

**2 cups crisp lettuce**
**2 cups water**
**2 cups green grapes with seeds**
**1 pear**

*Blend the crispy salad with water. Seed grapes and cut the pear into pieces. Add the remaining ingredients and blend again. Dilute with more water until desired consistency is reached.*

# Apple Pie Smoothie

With a little imagination, this smoothie resembles a scrumptious apple pie!

**2 handfuls of spinach**
**1–2 cups water**
**2 red apples**
**2 tbsp lúcuma powder**
**1–2 tsps cinnamon**

*Blend the spinach with 1 cup of water. Cut the apple into pieces. Add the remaining ingredients and mix again. Dilute with water until desired consistency is reached.*

# Green Christmas Smoothie

Sharon is a typical Christmas fruit. Don't worry if the fruit has some brown spots, as it's just a little sugar that has precipitated in the skin.

2 handfuls of kale
2–3 cups of water
1 large persimmon or two sharon fruit
1–2 tsps cinnamon

*Chop kale and mix with 1 cup of water. Cut persimmons/sharon into pieces and add together with cinnamon. Mix again. Add water until desired consistency is reached.*

# Papaya with Lime Smoothie

Papaya contains an extremely beneficial enzyme that helps our digestive system.

2 handfuls of spinach
1–2 cups water
¼ large papaya
½ lime juice

*Blend the spinach and 1 cup of water. Add chunks of papaya and lime juice and mix again. Add water until desired consistency is reached.*

# Ginger Green Smoothie

2 handfuls of kale
2 cups water
6 soaked figs, soaked 2–4 hours
½ inch ginger

*Chop the kale and mix with 1 cup of water. Add figs and peeled, chopped ginger and blend again. Add water until desired consistency is reached.*

# Green Creamy Apricot Smoothie

Dried apricots should be brown. Avoid buying the orange ones, which are sulfurized, meaning that sulfur has been added. This is done to inhibit bacteria and fungi and to preserve the color. However, this can also cause asthma.

1 cup nettle
1 cup spinach
½ cup of soaking water
1½ cup water
1 red apple
8 soaked apricots, soaked 2–4 hours

*Chop the nettles and mix with spinach, water, and the water from the apricots. Add pieces of apples and apricots, and mix again.*

# Col. Mustard Greens

**2 cups mustard greens**
**2–3 roma tomatoes**
**¼ avocado**
**1 small zucchini**
**1 lime**
**Favorite herbs to taste**

Blend with water to desired consistency.

*Works well with fresh oregano, basil, or dill, but feel free to experiment with other fresh herbs.*

# What-A-Lemon

2–4 cups watermelon

1 bunch watercress

1 roma tomato

½ lemon

1 tbsp olive oil

*Blend with ice to desired consistency.*

# Apple Sprouts

¼ of a small red onion
1 apple
1 pear
1 handful spinach
3–4 Brussels sprouts
Ginger to taste

*Blend with ice to desired consistency.*

# Sangria Blanca

1–2 white peaches (pitted)
1 cup rainier cherries (pitted)
1–2 white nectarines (pitted)
1 cup green grapes
6–10 endive leaves
3–5 mint leaves

*Blend with ice to desired consistency.*

# Mangomole

1 mango
1 peach
1 handful spinach
1 small bunch cilantro
¼ small onion
¼ avocado
½ yellow bell pepper
Jalapeño to taste
½ lemon (peeled)

*Blend with ice to desired consistency.*

# Gazpacho

1–2 roma tomatoes
½ red bell pepper
1 garlic clove
¼ small onion
1 handful cilantro
1 handful parsley
Jalapeño to taste
Tarragon to taste

*Blend with ice to desired consistency.*

# Cosmo Chiller

1–2 cups mustard greens
1 medium cucumber
1 cup frozen cranberries
1 lime (peeled)
½ lemon (peeled)
3–5 mint leaves

*Blend with ice to desired consistency.*

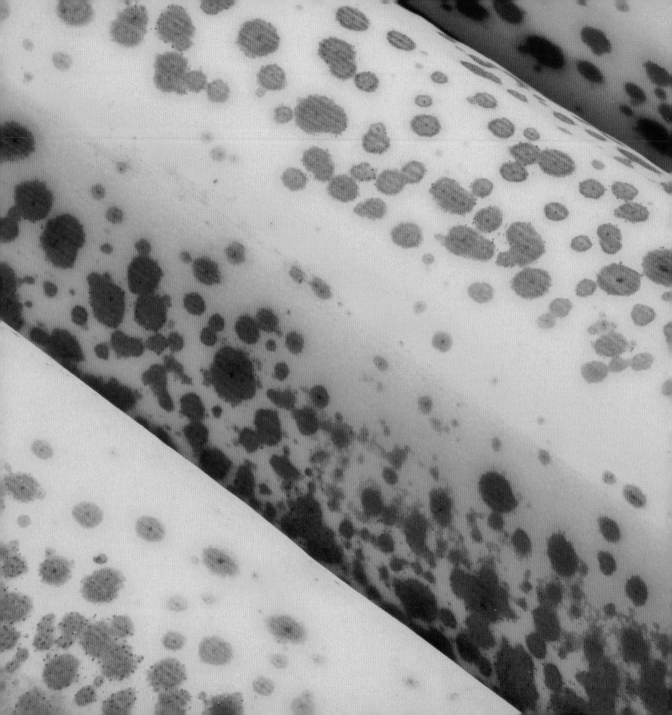

# Blue Banana Green Smoothie

1 frozen banana (ripe)
A handful of blueberries
2 inches of cucumber
1–2 cups of almond milk
A handful of baby spinach
1 tsp or less of honey
Ice

Optional Extras:
A handful of watercress

*Just throw all ingredients into the blender and starting low, blend well. Add a couple of ice cubes and turn up the blender.*

*Your smoothie will be crunchier if you are using almonds and water instead of almond milk.*

# Cacao Green Smoothie

1 frozen banana
Half an apple
1 tsp organic cacao powder
2 handfuls of baby spinach
1 heaped tsp of flax seed
1–2 cups of water

Optional Extras:
1 tsp cacao nibs (will be a little
    crunchy)
A few scrapes of a vanilla pod or a
    dash of vanilla extract (sugar-free)

*Blend all ingredients. This smoothie might be a little thin for your liking so if you want it thicker without adding any more ingredients, add some ice and blend. Otherwise, add an avocado.*

# Berry & Melon Green Smoothie

1 cup of raspberries

A few chunks of cantaloupe melon

1 banana

2 handfuls of spring greens

1–2 cups of water

Optional Extras:

A handful of sprouted broccoli or
 alfalfa seeds

*Put all the ingredients into the blender and starting low, work your way up to a high speed to really smooth out the spinach leaves.*

# Pineapple Detox Green Smoothie

A little grating of ginger
1 cup of pineapple
1 avocado
1 inch of cucumber
Several leaves of Romaine
    lettuce
Approx 2 cups of water

Optional Extras:
Some celery for further detoxing

*Start by blending the cucumber and pineapple with a little water. Then add the rest of the ingredients and speed up the blender to make smooth.*

# Zingy Spring Green Smoothie

½ squeezed lemon
2 handfuls of kale or spinach
1 apple
1 frozen banana
1 avocado
1 tbsp of chia seeds
Approx 1–2 cups of water
1 cup of ice

*Blend all ingredients apart from ice until smooth—then add the ice and smooth it up.*

# Berry Rocket Green Smoothie

1 frozen banana
1 cup of strawberries
1 cup of blackberries
1 handful of rocket or arugula lettuce
About 2 cups of coconut
   milk

*Put all the ingredients in blender and smooth it.*

# Pear Delicious Green Smoothie

2 pears
1 avocado
1 handful of lamb's lettuce
1 handful of coriander or cilantro
Approx 2 cups of water
1 tsp of maca (optional)
A little honey if extra sweetness is
   needed

*Blend all ingredients with ice until smooth. Taste and if your pears were not the really sweet kind, add a little honey.*

# Quick Green Smoothie

1 handful of spinach
1 small handful of parsley
1 frozen banana
1 papaya (seeds removed)
A couple ice cubes
1–2 cups of water

*Mix all ingredients in a blender until smooth. The parsley tastes quite strong, so add more banana if you are not used to it or make with just a sprig or two.*

# Quick Orange Breakfast Green Smoothie

2 large swiss chard leaves or lettuce
  leaves
1 whole oranges without seeds and
  peel
½ a grapefruit without seeds and peel
1 avocado
1 banana
Ice cubes
1 or 2 cups of water

Optional Extras:
A sprinkle of oats and 1 tbsp of vanilla
  rice protein powder

*Throw in all ingredients and blend—
then rush out the door!*

# Orange and Go Green Smoothie

1 orange
1 avocado
1 handful of spinach
1–2 cups of almond milk

**Optional Extras:**
Some lettuce and cucumber

*Blend all together and go!*

# Choco Passion Green Smoothie

1 frozen banana
2 handfuls spinach
1 passion fruit (the insides)
2 chunks of dark
   chocolate or 1 tsp of
   cocoa powder
2 cups of almond milk
   approx

*Mix all ingredients in a blender.*

# Sweet Green Smoothie

2 handfuls of kale
1 pear
1 banana
1–2 handfuls of dates
1 cup of water
Ice

*Blend everything together. Add a tsp of honey for an even sweeter taste.*

# Strawberry & Melon Delight Green Smoothie

2 cups of swiss chard
2 cups of watermelon
2 inches of cucumber
1 avocado
1 tsp of chia seed
1 squeeze of lemon
1 or 2 cups of water
Ice

*Mix all ingredients apart from the ice. Blend it well and then add the ice to cool it.*

# Tropical Green Smoothie

1 cup of pineapple chunks
1 cup of mango
1 handful of spinach
½ cup coconut milk, coconut water,
   or some coconut cream
Some water
Some ice

*Mix ingredients in a blender until smooth. Add ice at the end. Taste and add more of either coconut or water depending on your preference.*

# Wake Up Green Smoothie

1 cup of spinach
1 stalk celery
A chunk of cucumber
1 frozen banana
1 cup of raspberries
½–1 avocado
1 cup of cantaloupe melon chunks
1–2 cups of water

*Combine all ingredients and mix until smooth.*

# Fruity Power Green Smoothie

2 cups of swiss chard or kale
A few arugula (rocket) leaves
1 kiwi
1 banana
1 peach (pitted)
1 tsp of wheatgrass
1–2 cups of water

*Blend all ingredients together until smooth.*

# Breakfast Filler Green Smoothie

1 apple

½–1 avocado

1 cup of blueberries

2 handfuls of spinach

1 tsp of chocolate powder or a tbsp of cacao nibs

1 tbsp of instant oats (or pre-blended oats)

1 cup of water or green or white tea (chilled)

Several ice cubes

*Blend all ingredients together and then add the ice and crush.*

# Lunchtime Booster Green Smoothie

1 large slice of pineapple
3 leaves of romaine lettuce
½ avocado
1 handful of spinach leaves
1 frozen banana
1 tbsp of milled flax seed or chia seed
1 tsp of maca root
2 cups of water

*Blend all ingredients together until smooth. Add more banana for a thicker, sweeter smoothie.*

# Peach Punch

2 peaches
1 mango
1 bunch lettuce (red leaf or mixed)

*Remove the mango skin and all pits (stones). Blend with water or ice.*

**Optional Protein: Whey protein powder**

# Plumkin

1–2 spoonfuls pumpkin purée
1–2 plums (pitted)
1 large handful spinach
   cinnamon to taste
2 cups coconut water

Blend and add more coconut water as necessary.

*Add whole milk, chia seeds, or your favorite protein powder to make the perfect post-workout recovery green smoothie.*

**Optional Protein: Whole milk plain yogurt**

# Simply Sweet

2–4 kale leaves (de-stemmed)
1–2 cups strawberries
1 banana

*Blend with water and ice to desired consistency.*

**Optional Protein: Whey protein powder**

# Sweet Mint

1–2 large collard leaves
1 pear
1 kiwi (peeled)
1 cup blackberries
1 cup blueberries
3–6 mint leaves

*Blend with water and ice to desired consistency.*

**Optional Protein: Chia seeds**

# Piña Kale-ada

1 cup pineapple
1 orange (peeled)
2 leaves rainbow chard
2 kale leaves (stemmed)
1 banana
1 cup coconut milk

*Blend with ice to desired consistency.*

**Optional Protein: Whey protein powder**

# Wild Honey

3–4 large kale leaves (stemmed)
2–4 large basil leaves
1 cup blackberries
1 banana
1 tbsp honey

*Blend with water and ice to desired consistency.*

**Optional Protein: Whole milk plain yogurt**

# Chard Candy

2–4 chard leaves
1–2 cups red grapes
2–3 dates (pitted)
1 tbsp almond butter

*Blend with water and ice to desired consistency.*

**Optional Protein: Whole, raw milk**

# Cocoa Mo

2–3 kale leaves (stemmed)
1 handful mixed greens
1 apple
1 banana
1 tbsp almond butter
1–2 tbsp raw cocoa powder
   vanilla to taste

Blend with water and ice to desired consistency.

Vanilla extract is fine, but try to get find some vanilla beans and cut them open, scrape out the insides, and use that instead. They're delicious and you rid yourself of the alcohol used in extracts, however little there is.

**Optional Protein: Egg protein powder**

# Apple & Melon Smoothie

2 cups of honeydew melon, cut into pieces
1 apple
2 tbsp of organic live yogurt (greek yogurt is nice and thick)
1 tbsp lime juice
1 cup of water
Ice cubes

*Place all the ingredients into the blender and smooth it.*

# Coco Mango Smoothie

1 mango
1 banana
2 slices of pineapple juiced
1 tbsp of coconut cream or
1 cup of coconut milk or water
Water
Ice

*Just put the ingredients into the blender and whizz it!*

*Great for a quick fruit blast.*

# Melon Berry Yogurt Smoothie

½ a cantaloupe melon
1 cup of strawberries
½ banana
1 cup of live (healthy bacteria
   included) yogurt

*Mix all together in blender.*

# Grapefruit & Pineapple Diet Yogurt Smoothie

Several chunks of pineapple
1 small avocado
A few leaves of lettuce
½ a grapefruit
A big squeeze of lime
1 cup of low-fat live yogurt
Water to make less thick if necessary

*Blend all ingredients until smooth.*

# Pomegranate & Strawberries Smoothie

½ cup of fresh pomegranate juice

1 banana

A handful of strawberries (or mixed frozen berries)

1 large tbsp of crème fraîche or low-fat plain yogurt

1 tsp of honey (optional)

1 cup of water

Ice

*Put all ingredients into blender and mix until smooth.*

# Sweet Yogurt & Watermelon Smoothie

1 cup of greek yogurt with natural bacteria

1 tbsp of honey

2 cups of watermelon

½ cucumber (optional)

2 dates (optional)

Extra water if necessary

*Blend all together for a thick smoothie.*

# Cinnamon Apple Smoothie

2 apples
1 banana
1–2 tbsps of greek yogurt with natural
   bacteria
1 tsp of cinnamon
1 tsp of honey
1 cup approx of almond milk (or
   water and a handful of almonds for
   a thicker smoothie)
Ice

*Blend all ingredients together until smooth. Add a few cubes of ice as you go and check consistency.*

# PART III: JUICES

# The Quick and Dirty Flu Fighter

2 small–medium oranges, peeled
1 small grapefruit, peeled
½ lemon
1 Yellow or McIntosh apple (or any other sweet apple)
A small chunk of ginger

*Optional Additions:*
A handful of parsley

*Replacements:*
1 cup peeled pineapple for apple

# The Tart and Sweet Cooler

1 cup cranberries
½ cup raspberries
2 cups pineapple, peeled

*Optional Additions:*
½ lemon

*Replacements:*
Use either cranberries or raspberries if
you have only one.

# The Lola Dreaming

4 small Persian cucumbers
2 cups of baby spinach
A handful of mint
1 small yellow delicious
   apple
6–8 strawberries
1 lime
2 kiwis

*Optional Additions:*
A small chunk of ginger

*Replacements:*
Lemon for lime
Pear for apple


# The Berry Melon Heaven

10–12 strawberries
½–⅔ of a medium
   cantaloupe, peeled

*Optional Additions:*
A few chunks of pineapple

*Replacements:*
Honeydew for cantaloupe

# The Sweet Pear Sensation

2 small pears, any kind
1 medium sweet apple
2–4 stalks celery
½ lemon
A small chunk of ginger

*Optional Additions:*
3–4 strawberries or 4–5 raspberries

*Replacements:*
Pineapple for apple

# The Wake Me Up Morning Cocktail

2 cups fresh cranberries
2–3 medium carrots
A handful of cilantro
2 oranges, peeled
1 apple

*Optional Additions:*
2–4 strawberries or raspberries

*Replacements:*
Parsley or dill for cilantro
All oranges or all apples

# The Pomegranate Pow Wow

1 large pomegranate,
   peeled
½–1 lime
2 medium sweet apples,
   any kind

*Optional Additions:*
None

*Replacements:*
Lemon for lime

# The Sunrise in Paradise

2 mangoes, peeled
2 sweet delicious apples

*Optional Additions:*
2–4 strawberries
Ginger to taste

*Replacements:*
Pear for apple

# The Pink Silk

⅓ or ½ medium
   watermelon, peeled

*Optional Additions:*
A handful of fresh mint
½ lime

*Replacements:*
Basil or dill for mint leaves

# The Orange Ecstasy

3–4 medium carrots
2 oranges, peeled
A small chunk of ginger

*Optional Additions:*
½ lemon

# Antioxidant Rush

1 cup blueberries
1 cup cherries
2 apples

*Blueberries, cherries, and apples are all chock-full of antioxidants. All three are also anti-inflammatories, which can help with a wide range of conditions, including arthritis, chronic pain, heart disease, and even depression.*

# The Ruby Rapture

4 blood red oranges
8–10 strawberries

# Pear Delight

2 pears
2 cucumbers
½ lemon
½ cup strawberries or
    raspberries

*The pectin in pears is a type of fiber that is not lost when the fruit is juiced, making it good for colonic health. Pears also contain antioxidants that protect against brain aging. Berries are also full of antioxidants.*

# Tropical Punch

2 mangoes, peeled
1 cup pineapple
1 cup berries, any kind

*Mangoes are a good source of Vitamin C, Vitamin A, and quercetin, which helps to protect against cancer. Pineapple contains lots of Vitamin C and the enzyme bromelain, which reduces inflammation and supports digestive function. Berries are full of antioxidants.*

# Melon Refresher

¼ medium watermelon, flesh only
½ cantaloupe, flesh only
1 cup mint leaves

Watermelon contains Vitamins A, B1, B6, and C. Its high water content makes it incredibly hydrating and refreshing. Cantaloupe is high in Vitamins A and C and contains Vitamins B1, B6, and potassium. They help reduce anxiety and depression, and help fight intestinal and skin cancer, as well as cataracts. Mint leaves freshen breath and soothe the stomach.

# Very Berry

2 cups strawberries

2 cups blueberries

2 cups raspberries or blackberries

*Blueberries and blackberries contain anthocyanins, antioxidants that protect artery walls from damage caused by free radicals. Blackberries are also beneficial for skin. Strawberries are full of Vitamin C and antioxidants that protect the brain.*

# The Perfect Purifier

1 medium beet
¼ of cabbage head
2 Persian cucumbers
1 medium parsnip
A handful of parsley
1 large yellow or red sweet
    apple
1 lime

*Optional Additions:*
A handful (2–3) beet top greens to make it less sweet
Ginger and garlic to taste

*Replacements:*
Lemon for lime
Carrots for parsnip

# The Crystal Clean Lagoon

A large cucumber
A small handful of parsley
3–4 stalks of celery
3–4 medium carrots
1 small sweet pear
2 stalks and ¼ bulb of
    fennel
1 whole Belgian endive

*Optional Additions:*
A small handful of watercress
A small chunk of turmeric
1–2 cloves of garlic, peeled

*Replacements:*
More carrots for Belgian endive
Apple for pear
Any other cucumbers

# The Multi Nutri Juice

6 leaves of Swiss chard
⅔–1 beet
3–4 medium carrots
4 Roma tomatoes
A handful of parsley
1–2 small cucumbers
1 lemon
A chunk of ginger

*Optional Additions:*
1–2 cloves of garlic, peeled
A handful (2–3) beet top greens to make it less sweet

*Replacements:*
Celery for cucumbers
Kale for Swiss chard

# The Complete Winter Healer

4–5 leaves of Swiss chard
3–4 leaves of lettuce
2–3 medium carrots
1 medium beet
2–3 small cucumbers
2 Roma tomatoes
1 bunch watercress
½ lime or lemon
2 cloves garlic, peeled
A chunk of ginger

*Optional Additions:*
A handful (2–3) beet top greens to make it less sweet
A handful (2–3) carrot top greens to make it less sweet

*Replacements:*
Parsley for watercress
Spinach for Swiss chard

# The Highly Potent Palooza

4 stalks celery

1 cup spinach

3–4 broccoli florets and
    stems

½ bunch parsley

2 small Granny Smith
    green apples

2 cloves garlic

1 small chunk ginger

1 jalapeño pepper, seedless

*Optional Additions:*
1 small chunk turmeric

*Replacements:*
Cilantro for parsley
Carrot for apples

# The Super Detox Galore

6–8 leaves kale

4–6 stalks celery

1 whole Belgian endive

½ white onion

2 small red delicious
   apples

½ lemon or lime

1 chunk ginger

2 cloves of garlic

1 cayenne pepper

*Optional Additions:*
1 small handful watercress

*Replacements:*
Collard greens for kale
Cabbage for Belgian endive

# Red and Green Heavenly Concoction

3–4 medium carrots

6–8 leaves kale

⅓ fennel stalk and bulb

½ dill or mint bunch

3–4 Roma tomatoes

3–4 florets of broccoli

½ large Italian cucumber

1 lemon

*Optional Additions:*

½ bunch watercress

1–2 cloves garlic, peeled

*Replacements:*

Spinach for kale

Dill for cilantro

# The Hot Mamma Green Juice

2 Roma tomatoes

2–3 medium carrots

2 small parsnips

1 Italian cucumber

1 cup baby spinach

1 small handful cilantro

1 small handful parsley

¼ fennel

1 small cayenne pepper
(or spice powder to
taste)

*Optional Additions:*
Garlic and ginger to taste

*Replacements:*
More parsley for cilantro or vice versa
Jalapeño pepper for cayenne pepper
More carrots for the parsnips

# The Peaceful Warrior

24–26 leaves kale

2–4 medium carrots

1 cup of baby spinach

1 cup of arugula

2–4 broccoli florets and stem

3–4 leaves dandelion

2 medium oranges, peeled

*Optional Additions:*

Garlic and ginger to taste

*Replacements:*

Watercress for dandelion

Romaine lettuce for arugula

# Excitement in Your Mouth Juice

2 sweet potatoes, peeled

3–4 carrots

1 small cayenne pepper
(or cayenne pepper
powder to taste)

*Optional Additions:*
1–2 carrots

*Replacements:*
Apples for carrots

# The Feast of a Champion

1 sweet potato, peeled

2–3 Roma tomatoes

1 small beet

2 medium carrots

2–3 broccoli florets and stem

A handful of parsley

½ white or purple onion

1 small chunk ginger

2 cloves garlic

*Optional Additions:*
1 small chunk of turmeric

*Replacements:*
Celery for broccoli
Apple for tomato

# The Whole Enchilada

3–4 leaves kale

3–4 leaves Romaine
   lettuce

1 cup spinach

1 cup arugula

A handful of parsley

A handful of basil

A handful of dandelion

1 cup pineapple

8–10 strawberries

1 small chunk ginger

*Optional Additions:*

1 small chunk of turmeric

1 jalapeño pepper

*Replacements:*

Green collards for kale or spinach

# Rad-ish Radish

2–3 kale leaves (remove stems)

¼ English cucumber

4 medium radish bulbs (with greens)

Fresh ginger to taste

¼ cup water

Peel ginger root and juice all, adding more water if necessary.

*The spiciness of the radish and ginger are only slightly cooled down by the cucumber. A great drink to clear out the respiratory system or for those with seasonal allergies.*

*Add some bee pollen and double the allergy-fighting effects. You can even give it an Asian twist by substituting daikon radish for the standard red bulb.*

# Broccolean

1 small crown broccoli
1 bunch parsley
4 carrots
1 medium cucumber

Juice.

*An easier taste for a more seasoned juice-goer, Broccolean administers your daily dose of vegetables and helps to work your way to a slimmer figure and a healthier heart in just one glass.*

*Though carrots are high in sugar, they also provide a super jolt to the immune system, helping to fight illness and promote overall health. Parsley delivers a rich source of antioxidants, making this an all-around beauty beverage.*

# The Ultimate Pineapple-Kale Blast

6–8 large leaves of kale
 with stem
½ large Italian cucumber
½ bunch parsley
2–2½ cups of pineapple
 chunks, peeled
¾–1 cup strawberries

*Optional Additions:*
A handful of fresh mint

*Replacements:*
Any other cucumber
Swiss chard for kale
Either a sweet apple for the strawberries or pineapple but not both

# The Vitamin C Minty Rush

3–4 cups baby spinach
A handful of parsley
2 small delicious apples
2 medium oranges, peeled
6–8 stems fresh mint
1 lemon
1 small chunk of ginger

*Optional Additions:*
1–2 small Persian cucumbers

*Replacements:*
Use all oranges or all apples

# The Dapper Dan

4 stalks Bok choy

2–4 broccoli crowns with
short stalks

4–6 leaves of kale

1 cup green grapes

2–3 small Granny Smith
apples

1 lemon

*Optional Additions*
1 small chunk of ginger

*Replacements:*
Lime for lemon
Spinach or collard greens for kale

# The Emerald Deluxe

2–3 cups of baby or
   regular spinach
3–4 stalks of celery
3–4 small Persian
   cucumbers
1 cup green or red grapes
1 large Granny Smith
   apple
A small chunk of ginger

*Optional Additions:*
A handful of fresh mint or dill

*Replacements:*
Any other cucumber
Collard greens or kale for spinach

# The Green Explosion

6–8 leaves of collard greens

1 medium Italian cucumber

A large handful of parsley

2 medium Granny Smith apples

1 medium orange, peeled

1 small jalapeño pepper, seedless

½ lime

*Optional Additions:*

2 cloves of garlic, peeled

A chunk of ginger

*Replacements:*

Any other cucumber

Spinach or kale for collard greens

# The Shanti Om Elixir

A handful of cilantro

2–3 stalks celery

A small head of Romaine lettuce

4–6 leaves of Swiss chard

1 small red apple

1 medium yellow apple

½ lime

1 kiwi

*Optional Additions:*

Garlic and ginger to taste

*Replacements:*

Spinach for lettuce

Parsley for cilantro

Any other sweet apple to replace

# The Frothy Monkey Juice

⅓ of a large fennel

A bunch of mint

A small handful of
   watercress

4 large leaves of kale

A chunk of ginger

1–1½ cups of pineapple

8–10 strawberries

*Optional Additions:*

A chunk of turmeric

1–2 cloves of garlic, peeled

*Replacements:*

Spinach or collard greens for kale

A handful of dill or mint for fennel

# The Green Goddess

37–38 large kale leaves

1½–2 cups baby or regular
   spinach

12 strawberries

1 Granny smith medium–
   large apple

A handful of mint

¼ fennel, bulb and stalk

1 lime

*Optional Additions*

A handful of dill

*Replacements:*
Lemon for lime
Cilantro or parsley for mint

# The Smooth Sensation

3–4 large leaves of Swiss chard

3–4 broccoli florets and stems

A small handful of parsley

½ large Italian cucumber

1 lemon

6–8 strawberries

2 small orchard apples

*Optional Additions:*

1–2 cloves of garlic, peeled

2–4 leaves basil

*Replacements:*

Any other cucumber

Any other sweet apple

Spinach or kale for Swiss chard

# The Zen Dragonfly

2–3 cups baby or regular spinach

A small head of Romaine lettuce

1 medium pear

1 medium Granny Smith apple

8–10 strawberries

*Optional Additions:*

Ginger and garlic to taste

*Replacements:*

Raspberries for strawberries

Pears for apples and vice versa

# The Emerald Fantasy

1 grapefruit, peeled

1 orange, peeled

1 Honey Crisp (or any other) apple

2 stalks and ¼ bulb of fennel

½ bunch basil

½ bunch cilantro

1 large Italian cucumber

1 small chunk of raw turmeric

*Optional Additions:*
Ginger and garlic to taste

*Replacements:*
Any other cucumber
All grapefruit or all orange

# The Unbelievably Creamy Lush Dream

1 large sweet potato, peeled
2 medium red apples
3–4 medium size carrots

*Optional Additions:*
1 jalapeño pepper, seedless

*Replacements:*
Any other sweet apple
Cayenne pepper for jalapeño

# The Perfect Simple Essence

2 Roma or other type tomatoes
3–4 carrots
1 small yellow or red sweet bell pepper, seedless
2 Persian cucumbers
1 small chunk ginger

*Optional Additions:*
1 small handful parsley
1 clove garlic, peeled

*Replacements:*
Any other cucumber

# The Sexy Sassy Surprise

3–4 carrots
1 medium head of
   Romaine lettuce
8–10 strawberries
1 medium or large pear
1 handful of fresh basil
½–1 lime

*Optional Additions:*
1–2 cloves garlic, peeled

*Replacements:*
Any other lettuce except iceberg
Lemon for lime
Mint or fennel for basil

# The Yellow Sunset

2–2½ cups Baby or regular
   spinach
¼ fennel bulb and stalk
2 small oranges, peeled
1–1½ cups mango, peeled

*Optional Additions:*
A handful of fresh mint or basil

*Replacements:*
Apple for mango

# Cool Slaw

1 crown broccoli
½ small red cabbage
2 carrots
1 lemon (peeled)
1 green apple
Ginger to taste

Peel ginger root and juice all. Serve over ice.

A fresh-tasting summer delight perfect for parties by the pool, barbecues, and picnics at the park. Besides being the ideal accompaniment to any afternoon outside, Cool Slaw brings a lot to the picnic table.

Broccoli's cancer-fighting properties combat the carcinogens introduced to your meat from that smokey grill. Ginger works to settle stomachs and has long been a remedy for heartburn from those summer snacks. Serve with a few extra apples in your favorite punch bowl.

# The Tummy Rub

This green juice is an efficient cleanser and tonic of the hardworking yet delicate digestive system. Drink it half an hour before a heavy meal, as it stimulates your gut and gets it ready for action. You can also replace a meal with it if you're feeling heavy from a previous binge.

**1 cup pineapple chunks**
**½ fennel bulb**
**½ cucumber**
**1 cup spinach**
**½ lemon**

Process all the ingredients in a juicer and serve.

Fennel has an aniseed flavor and, similar to that seed, aids digestion and prevents gas. It is also known to be a diuretic, reduce inflammation, and prevent cancer. As a food, only the round bulb is usually used, but for juicing use the bulb, stalks, and leaves. Everything goes.

# 4 Carrot Gold

4 carrots
2 large kale leaves
1 bok choy bulb
1 golden apple
Ginger to taste

Peel ginger root and juice all. Serve over ice.

*Rich, I say, rich! Rich in vitamins, color, and in flavor, that is. Adding apple has always been a great way to balance out the grainy sweetness of carrots and still deliver the unbeatable shot of beta-carotene you get from them.*

*Bok choy's health-promoting compounds are better preserved when it is left uncooked, and what better way to maximize these rich health benefits. Break out the blender and have yourself a gold rush.*

# Red Queen

2 kale leaves
1 medium beet
1 gala apple
¼ red cabbage
1 bunch red grapes

Juice.

*Long live the queen. Super sweet, sassy, and deep, dark red, Red Queen is one smart drink. Grape juice promotes brain health and memory function. Red cabbage is rich in iodine, which also promotes proper brain and nervous system function. One sip and you'll be singing the Red Queen's "Off with the cabbage head!" Just remember what the dormouse said, "Feed your head!"*

# Beetle Juice

1 yellow bell pepper
1 Fuji apple
1 small crown broccoli
1 small beet
½ sweet potato
1 handful parsley
2 carrots

Juice.

*Saying it three times in succession may not raise the dead, but it will certainly raise your spirits and your energy levels. Bell pepper is a natural immune booster and coupled with broccoli, you've got yourself one helluva free-radical fighter. Eating sweet root vegetables like beets and sweet potato helps calm sugar cravings, so put down that donut and drink your veggies.*

# Hot Rocket

2 Gala apples
2 handfuls of arugula
1 handful of cilantro
2 cups coconut water/
  milk
1 smidgen of jalapeño
  (to taste)
Soy sauce to taste

Juice and mix with coconut water and soy sauce.

*This one is a bit different. We've got very bold and spicy flavors here. The coconut water, jalapeño, and salty soy sauce combine to give Hot Rocket a kind of Thai flavor while the cilantro brings back the Mexican flare.*

*Cilantro is also great for removing heavy metals from the bloodstream and jalapeños can raise your body temperature thereby increasing your metabolic rate. The healthy fats in the coconut milk will allow increase in mineral absorption from the arugula and cilantro.*

# Dande-Lemon

1 bunch dandelion greens
1 bulb radicchio
Ginger to taste
1 lemon (juiced, to taste)
Dash cayenne

Juice and mix in cayenne.

*The ginger, lemon, and cayenne do a great job of taming the bitterness of the blood- and liver-purifying dandelion greens. This is like a suped-up lemonade. Master Cleanse aficionados will appreciate the lemon juice–cayenne pairing, which increases your body's fat-burning power and strengthens your immune system. Not much else to say except, it's really dandy.*

# Veggie-All

1 beet
2 stalks celery
1 green bell pepper
1 large cucumber
Lemon (juiced, to taste)
1 tsp olive oil

Juice and mix (shake) with olive oil.

*Olive oil is a phytonutrient powerhouse and also helps the body absorb the many vitamins and minerals in the other vegetables.*

*You might want to play with the amount of green bell pepper here because sometimes the flavor can completely take over, or perhaps use a yellow or red pepper since they have a fruitier flavor. Sometimes I even add a couple of carrots to sweeten the lot.*

# Green King

1 crown broccoli
1 green apple
1 bunch green grapes
2 handfuls spinach
2 large leaves collard
  greens

Juice.

*Where would we be without a solid green drink? I introduce you to a king and his crown . . . of broccoli?*

*Absolutely. Broccoli, the miracle food, packs the most nutritional punch of any vegetable, and it meets your complete fiber need providing both soluble and insoluble fiber. Green grapes are a natural antihistamine and despite their tiny stature, they really add quite a bit of sweetness. A juice fit for a king.*

# Rocket Fuel

2 oz. (juiced) wheatgrass
   (or kale)
2 handfuls arugula
1–2 oranges (peeled)

Juice.

*All the energy and alertness provided by a shot of espresso without the shakes and eventual crash—this is what you can find in wheatgrass.*

*Wheatgrass is a high-alkaline, nutritionally dense green with a fairly potent flavor that some people have a hard time acclimating to; that's why you'll often find it paired with fresh orange slices at your local fresh juice bar. Not to mention it infuses the already high vitamin content with a significant amount of immune-boosting Vitamin C.*

# Green Clean

1 lime
1 lemon
1 large cucumber
1 handful basil
1 handful mint
2 handfuls spinach
Ginger to taste

Juice.

*This one begs to be put into a giant ice-filled punch bowl and ladled into frosty glasses poolside. You'll never know your body is detoxifying as you gulp this delicious summer treat. Some folks may find it a bit too sour, so try adding an apple or two if that's the case.*

*Not only do we have great flavor, high amounts of vitamins, minerals, and antioxidants, Green Clean is one of the most aromatically appealing drinks in this book. Crisp, clean, refreshing.*

# Ginger Snap

3–4 handfuls spinach
1 small anise bulb
Ginger to taste
3–4 dates
1 cup frozen cherries
  (optional)

Juice spinach, anise, and ginger. Toss in a blender with dates and, for a Ginger Roy Rogers, add cherries. Blend. Serve over ice.

*This is practically a liquid dessert. Anise is great for digestion and paired with ginger, this drink is a perfect after-meal delight. The anise has a sophisticated licorice flavor that when paired with the sweetness of the dates makes for a dreamy combination.*

*The ginger adds a nice bite that helps steer you away from diabetic shock. Throw in a few frozen cherries to brighten it up or dare I say, add a scoop of sugar-free coconut ice cream for a float you won't soon forget.*

# Blimey Mary!

2 medium tomatoes
2 celery stalks
1 bunch watercress
1–2 green onions (to taste)
1–2 carrots
1 lime (peeled)
Tabasco and pepper to
    taste

Juice. Add Tabasco and pepper.

*A more savory flavor profile, the Blimey has heat, spice, and a double shot of nutrients. Celery, known as the zero-calorie vegetable, yields a sweet, savory, and slightly salty taste while the watercress and green onion spice it up a bit.*

*Tomatoes, the highlight of this drink, accounts for the slight sweet flavor and contains high levels of lycopene, known to fight against a list of cancers.*

*Add a dash of Tabasco for an extra kick and you've got a simple way to get that tomato juice taste without adding an unnecessary amount of sodium to your diet.*

# Cold Killah

3–4 leaves purple kale
1 lemon (peeled)
Ginger to taste
1 clove garlic
45–50 drops echinacea
2–3 carrots
1 sweet red bell pepper

Juice. Add echinacea and mix.

*Packed with Vitamin C, Cold Killah is the perfect cure or preemptive strike during cold season. Not only is echinacea known to boost the immune system, but so does the high amount of beta-carotene from both the carrots and red bell pepper.*

*Juicing to fight colds and illness is always a healthier and tastier alternative to those powdered cure packets any day. Sensing that tickle in your throat? Juice up a batch of Cold Killah, it'll stop that cold bug in its tracks.*

# Gold 'n' Delicious

2 Golden Delicious apples
1 kiwi (peeled)
2 cups chopped mustard
   greens
2 stalks celery
1 peach (pitted)

Juice.

Another dark green with heavy cancer-fighting properties, mustard greens have a spicier flavor profile than most others in the cruciferous family. Though these greens are often cooked, when juiced, their health benefits are amplified.

Toss in some sweet apples, peach, and kiwi to cut the spice and add a dose of vitamins and antioxidants and you've got yourself one delicious drink.

# Beet the Blues

If you're an '80s kid, the color of this juice may bring back memories of grape flavored chewing gum rolls that came in hard plastic containers. Thankfully, in this case the cheerful color is not the result of scary chemi-cals and colorings, but of all the goodness stored inside blueberries and beets instead.

1 beet (with leaves, optional)
1 cup blueberries
½ romaine lettuce
2 celery ribs
½ cucumber
½ apple
½–1 inch piece ginger, peeled

Process all the ingredients in a juicer and serve.

When using beets, don't discard the greens. They are as good as the roots, and have a similar earthy flavor. In fact, beets were originally grown for their leaves, not their roots. You can use yellow or white beets, but nothing is more stunning than the intense magenta color that regular beets give to any juice.

# Pink Magic Woman

The color of this juice is so pretty and intense that it literally feels like you're drinking an elixir of youth and beauty every time you have a glass. Besides using ginger to give it a spicy and warming tingle, you can add freshly squeezed orange juice, or substitute the strawberries with raspber-ries for a more acidic taste.

**1 beet**
**1 cup strawberries**
**½ romaine lettuce**
**½ cucumber**
**½-inch piece ginger, peeled**

Process the ingredients in a juicer and serve.

You should try to add beets to your diet as frequently as possible, especially in the winter, when they are in season. However, be careful not to overdo them because their sugar content is high. The same advice goes for carrots and fruits from the sweeter varieties: a little bit, often, goes a long way.

# Beet-er Dandelion

This intensely colored and flavored juice is not for the faint hearted. The bitterness of dandelion may put sweetness seekers off this drink, but for me, its superior detoxifying properties more than make up for it. No pain, no gain.

2 dandelion leaves
1 beet
1 carrot
½ cucumber
½–1 lemon
½ Granny Smith apple (optional)

Juice all the ingredients and serve.

If you want the real hardcore version of this juice, have it without the apple. The beets and carrots already are rich in sugar, and more fruit only adds to it. However, if you really need it, you can add the fruit to get the benefits of the dandelion leaves past your taste buds.

# Save the Veggies

This original juice was created to recycle some leftover tomatoes and spin-ach that were being ignored in the fridge for a couple days. The sweetness added by the berries and pineapple water gave these veggies a 180° turn.

1 cup berries
1 tomato
1–2 cups spinach
½–1 cup pineapple water

Juice the first three ingredients.

Mix with the pineapple water and serve.

Tomatoes are part of the nightshades group of foods, which have somewhat of a bad rep, blaming them for having toxins that cause inflammation and pain. Defenders of nightshades, which also include potatoes, peppers, and eggplants, claim that the benefits far outweigh any potential problems caused by such low doses of these toxins. Our verdict? As long as you're not overdoing it, you can reap positive benefits from mostly anything.

# Forever Young

The strong cilantro flavor in this refreshing juice is perfectly balanced by the sweetness of the carrots and the acidity of the lemon. The result is a truly enjoyable drink that will flush a huge amount of toxins out of your body. This is a recipe you may want to go back to again and again, not only for how much your liver loves it, but also for how much you do.

½ cucumber
1 large carrot
1 cup cilantro
Juice of ½ lemon

Juice the cucumber, carrots and cilantro.

Squeeze the lemon into the juice and stir.

Who needs a cold beer when it's hot and muggy outside? The minerals in this juice will quench your thirst better than any other drink.

# Lettuce Sleep

This calming potion is an amazing pre-sleep meal or snack, as both apples and lettuce are incredibly relaxing. The ingredients in this juice will also keep you satiated, narrow your waist line, and help your liver detoxify, all in one sip. Happy snoozing!

1 Granny Smith apple
½ cucumber
1 romaine lettuce
4 mint sprigs
½ lime

Process all the ingredients in a juicer and serve.

When you're not going to use the whole lettuce head, start taking layers from the outside in, instead of cutting it in half. This way you will keep it from turning brown where the cut is. Store it in the fridge, inside a plastic bag.

# PART IV: PROBIOTIC DRINKS

# Komucha Recipes

## About Kombucha

Kombucha is a naturally bubbly (or "effervescent") probiotic drink. It originated in Northeast China then made its way to Russia. Kombucha was then brought to Germany, followed by the rest of Europe and the world. Kombucha is made from a living organism called a SCOBY, which stands for Symbiotic Culture of Bacteria and Yeast. A SCOBY is often referred to as a "mushroom" or "the mother." It grows, multiplies, ferments, and feeds off tea and sugar. The probiotics and yeast eat the sugar, which ferments the beverage and results in a drink that is acidic, probiotic-rich, and mildly alcoholic. Just like all recipes in this book, it is important to take precautions when fermenting living organisms.

Kombucha contains acetic acid, which is a mild natural antibiotic. Because of the acidity of kombucha, bad strains of bacteria cannot grow in the culture, as the environment is not optimal for survival or reproduction. In this way, the good bacteria thrive while the bad bacteria have no fighting chance. Kombucha also contains lactic acid, and is rich in B vitamins, folate, and antioxidants.

It is stated that kombucha can aid in digestion, increase energy, manage hunger, and can create pH balance in the digestive tract. There is still a great deal of debate on whether there is scientific proof to support these health claims. It is important to keep in mind that this book makes no claim that kombucha will improve health nor will the alleged benefits apply to all individuals. Regardless, kombucha tastes great and most people report that it gives their digestive system regularity and makes them feel good.

If you have purchased kombucha or any other form of probiotic beverage from the grocery store, you have no doubt noticed how expensive it is. I began brewing kombucha because I was drinking store-bought kombucha every day and the cost was becoming unreasonable for my budget. With a few small start-up costs, I began brewing kombucha, which is an investment that has paid for itself hundreds of times over.

Brewing kombucha may seem very daunting and intimidating at first, but don't let the long list of instructions fool you. It's actually very easy to make homemade kombucha, but I want to emphasize the importance of brewing safely by providing detailed instructions.

## How to Start

To brew kombucha, you need several kitchen tools plus a kombucha SCOBY in starter liquid. Starter liquid is simply unflavored homebrewed kombucha. There are many online sources from which you can purchase a SCOBY. I caution you to read reviews and talk to others who have purchased from the specific suppliers you are looking at because the quality of some SCOBY suppliers is more reliable than others. If you do choose to purchase your SCOBY online, make sure you begin brewing as soon as possible because the SCOBY will already be in slight shock from traveling and it is important to get it fed and in a healthy environment.

# Keeping Your SCOBY and Kombucha Healthy

What does it mean to keep a SCOBY healthy? I will touch on this throughout the list of instructions, but essentially it means the following:

1. *Feeding the SCOBY* a mixture of tea and sugar; 100 percent black tea works best for brewing kombucha, but you may also use 100 percent green tea. Fancy teas typically contain peels and other ingredients that are not conducive to brewing kombucha. Plain black tea works great.

2. *Keeping it out* of the sunlight in a dark place: a closet shelf works as an excellent home for brewing kombucha or jun.

3. *Keeping it covered* while still allowing it to breathe: a kitchen towel or cheesecloth secured by a stretchy rubber band works perfectly to keep out the bugs.

4. *Giving it an optimal* temperature range (between 75° and 85° Fahrenheit).

5. *Keeping the SCOBY* moist with starter liquid. I recommend maintaining at least two inches of starter liquid for every one inch of SCOBY.

If you choose to purchase your SCOBY online, make sure you begin brewing a batch as soon as you receive it, as the SCOBY will be in shock.

## Giving One of Your SCOBYs Away

With each new batch of kombucha you brew, a new SCOBY will form. While it is perfectly okay to allow the SCOBY to continue to grow, I find my SCOBY looks healthiest when it is three inches thick or less. You can peel off layers of your kombucha SCOBY and give them to your friends or family.

To do so, add starter liquid (which is simply kombucha) and a SCOBY to a plastic bag. Seal well and make sure the SCOBY lays flat and is out of direct sunlight while it is transported.

Because the SCOBY will be in shock from traveling, it is important to remove it from the bag as soon as possible so it can breathe. Inform the person you give the SCOBY to that they should brew a batch of kombucha as soon as they get the SCOBY home.

## Fermenting Kombucha

Like any fermentation process, there needs to be food for the active probiotics and yeasts to feed off. For kombucha, food is tea and sugar. Each batch of kombucha you brew, a new SCOBY will form and the SCOBY will grow to the width of the container it is in. For instance, once you are on your fifth batch of kombucha, you will have five layers of SCOBY. As you brew, you can allow your SCOBY to grow, and you don't need to discard it until it reaches more than three inches thick.

In addition to tea and sugar, kombucha requires an optimal temperature range to flourish. Between 75° and 85° Fahrenheit is the optimal temperature range for brewing kombucha. While it is generally okay for kombucha to experience temperatures outside that range, you will notice a difference in the strength of the kombucha if it is brewing below 70° or above 80°. A lower temperature may require a longer brewing time, whereas a higher temperature will make the fermentation process go faster. Too warm a temperature can kill the probiotics.

The fun part about brewing kombucha is flavoring it. It is perfectly fine to drink the kombucha you brew plain and not put it through a secondary fermentation; however, for the purpose of your kombucha enjoyment, I have included multiple recipes that you can use to make fizzy, sweet kombucha that can be enjoyed throughout the year. Note that kombucha should be flavored after it has gone through the first fermentation, as putting anything other than sweetened tea in a SCOBY's environment can change the structure and health of the probiotics.

## What is Secondary Fermentation and How Does it Work?

Secondary fermentation involves fermenting a beverage that has already been fermented for a second time. When you brew kombucha for the first fermentation, the bacteria and yeast feed off the sugar and tea that you give them. Once all of the "food" has been consumed by the probiotics, they are ready for more. This is where secondary fermentation comes in.

Immediately after the first fermentation (before you refrigerate the kombucha), you can add additional tea and water to begin a secondary fermentation. You can also add various fruits, herbs, and non-toxic flowers to flavor your kombucha to your liking. Once you have added additional ingredients, you can then bottle the kombucha and leave it in a dark place at room temperature for two to three days and the kombucha will continue fermenting.

Since the bottles are sealed, some pressure will build and the beverage will then become effervescent (or naturally carbonated). Similar to the first fermentation, the more sugar you add, the longer it will take the probiotics to process it. If you want your kombucha sweet, you can either add more sugar (cane sugar or fruit) than necessary or only allow the second fermentation to last one or two days versus two to three. Fermentation slows when you refrigerate the kombucha but does not stop completely.

Now here comes the really cool part! Depending on what you use for the secondary fermentation, you will end up with varying levels of effervescence. I found that more acidic fruit yields a more effervescent kombucha. I have also found that leaving fruit pulp inside the bottles during the secondary fermentation results in more effervescence. Additionally, allowing the sealed bottles to refrigerate for at least twenty-four hours before popping the bottle open will yield a more effervescent kombucha.

To summarize: to get the most effervescent kombucha (if that is what you're going for), use an acidic fruit for the secondary fermentation process, leaving the pulp inside the bottles and allowing the bottles to sit for two to three days at room temperature. Then refrigerate the bottles for one to two days before drinking.

Berries, apricots, and pineapple have resulted in the spunkiest kombucha in my experience. Remember to shorten the length of the secondary fermentation if you desire a sweeter (less dry) kombucha.

Because pressure and effervescence builds during the secondary fermentation, it is very important that you point the bottles away from your face when you open them. If you are using good quality flip-cap bottles, it is likely that you will have a batch or two of kombucha that will fizz out of the bottle when opened, similar to opening a can of soda after it's been rolling around in the back of your car). Just be sure to open the bottles over the sink and never point them at your face or anything breakable. Do not ever give a small child a bottle of kombucha to open.

## Kombucha and Allergies and/or Detox

A very small portion of the population is allergic to kombucha. The exact science behind the allergy is unknown. Similar to doing a juice cleanse, some people go through a detoxification after drinking kombucha. This may be perceived as an allergic reaction but it could be the body ridding itself of toxins. Symptoms of detox include headache, more frequent than usual bowel movements, runny nose, or even vomiting. Should you experience any of these symptoms, it is best to consult a doctor before attempting to consume any more kombucha.

It is not recommended to drink homemade kombucha on an empty stomach. If your stomach ever hurts after drinking kombucha, it could mean one of three things—your batch is bad (unlikely, unless you notice mold and/or the batch tastes abnormal), you drank too much, or your kombucha is too strong. Depending on the ingredients added for secondary fermentation, it is possible for people to have a negative reaction to one flavor and have no problem with other flavors.

## Taking a Break Between Batches of Kombucha

By no means do you have to continue brewing kombucha forever and ever with no break between batches. Once your SCOBY is growing, you may consider peeling off one of the SCOBYs and using it in an additional jug to brew a higher volume of kombucha at one time. With that said, you may end up with more kombucha than you feel you need or you may simply get sick of brewing. Never fear, you don't have to throw your kombucha SCOBY out! You can store your kombucha SCOBY in the same way you would store kombucha that is brewing: in a jar covered with cheesecloth bound with a rubber band.

Be sure there is plenty of starter fluid to keep the SCOBY moist. One inch of starter fluid for every one inch of SCOBY works well. You will need this starter fluid to keep your SCOBY alive and also to start your next batch when you are ready to brew again. If you go several weeks between batches, check on the SCOBY every once in a while to be sure it still has ample starter fluid.

## Cleaning Your Tools

It is very important that everything you use that touches the SCOBY and/or kombucha be properly sanitized. You can sanitize your tools in the dishwasher, or with hot, soapy water, or by soaking them in distilled white vinegar for a couple minutes. If there is harmful bacteria on any of the tools you use, it can potentially contaminate your kombucha.

You do not need to clean the jug that you use to brew kombucha between batches. I do, however, recommend that you clean it periodically (I clean mine every three to five batches). To clean the jug, pour all of the kombucha liquid into bottles (if you haven't already) except for a small amount of fluid to act as starter for your next batch. Place the SCOBY and starter fluid into a glass or stainless steel bowl and cover with a kitchen towel. Fill the jug with very hot, soapy water and use a sponge to get every last bit of kombucha culture out. I repeat this process multiple times to ensure my jug is sanitary.

Distilled white vinegar acts as a sanitizing agent, so you can use vinegar to clean the jug, as well. Pour about ½ cup of distilled white vinegar in the jug and slosh it around for a minute or two. Pour the vinegar out. You can either rinse the jug with clean spring/well water or simply leave it as is. A little bit of residual vinegar will not harm your SCOBY.

Now you can start another batch of kombucha by first adding your tea/sugar mixture to the jug and then carefully (and with clean hands) pouring the starter liquid and SCOBY back in the jug. Secure the opening with cheesecloth bound by a rubber band.

## Flavoring Your Kombucha

While it is not necessary to add flavors to kombucha once it has finished its primary fermentation, experimenting with flavors is by far the most fun part of brewing kombucha! There are a myriad of options for giving your kombucha flavor, spunk, and fizz. Fresh fruit and herbs are my favorite ingredients to add before secondary fermentation to ensure the beverage will be bubbly, just the right amount of sweetness, and full of added health benefits.

One-hundred percent fruit juices are also effective for secondary fermentation, although not to the same extent as fresh fruit. Kombucha likes fruit pulp and tends to be much fizzier when fruit pulp is added for secondary fermentation. For every one gallon of kombucha, 1 cup of fruit juice can be added for secondary fermentation.

It is important to be mindful of the strength of your kombucha. If your kombucha is strong (meaning its pH is lower than 2.5), dilute it with additional sweetened tea along with fruit or other ingredients prior to the secondary fermentation. This ensures there will be enough sugar and tea for the probiotics to feed on for an effective secondary fermentation and will also ensure the kombucha is safe for consumption.

Typically for a gallon of strong kombucha, steeping 4 teabags in 4 cups of water and adding some sugar (¼ to ½ cup) is sufficient to dilute it, but depending on the strength, a higher amount of freshly brewed tea may be used. Always cool the tea (and any other hot ingredients) to room temperature before mixing it with kombucha because excessive heat will kill the probiotics.

Because you will need to save starter liquid (for every one inch of SCOBY, I typically save one to two inches of starter liquid) and also to leave some room at the top of the jar so that the liquid doesn't spill over when the jar is moved, you will not get a true gallon when brewing 1 gallon of kombucha. The liquid yield is closer to ¾ gallon or less depending on how thick your SCOBY is. Similarly, when brewing kombucha in a 2-gallon jug, you will not get a full 2 gallons of kombucha. Most individuals brew either 1 gallon or 2 gallons of kombucha at a time, so I chose to focus my kombucha recipes on the 1-gallon batches. This means each recipe in this section calls for ¾ gallon of kombucha, but you can easily double the recipes if desired.

## Don't Be Surprised If . . .

Don't be surprised when small SCOBYs form in the bottles during secondary fermentation. Because the probiotics and yeast continue to ferment, they form a colony during secondary fermentation, which is clear, gooey, and typically the size of a quarter. If you drink one by accident, nothing bad will happen, although the slimy texture going down your throat is not desirable for most people. Prior to drinking kombucha, use a fine strainer to catch whatever bacteria and yeast colonies (and/or fruit pulp that was added for flavor) have formed so that you can enjoy a SCOBY-free beverage.

Don't be surprised when your SCOBY forms long brown strings underneath it. These are colonies of yeast and they look kind of like kelp. They are completely normal and do not need to be cleaned out or removed. Some people mistakenly think these furry-looking strings are evidence that the SCOBY has gone bad, when they're actually evidence of a healthy SCOBY.

# A Note About Safety

Making homemade kombucha can be risky if you are not careful. If you are new to making kombucha, please seek multiple sources to educate yourself about the process of brewing. It is very important to keep all instruments used in the process of making kombucha clean and to keep the SCOBY healthy. It is also important to avoid using ceramic or plastic for storing kombucha.

Use common sense and know that there is risk associated with fermentation. If you see a single spot of mold, abandon ship—throw out your whole SCOBY, discard all kombucha liquid, and completely sanitize the jar or jug you used to brew. Mold on kombucha looks similar to bread mold—it's usually circular, white or green, and fuzzy. I have made countless batches of kombucha and allowed my SCOBYs to sit in their starter liquid for a month at a time and I've never encountered mold. Have faith that as long as you follow the instructions and keep your SCOBY in a healthy environment, it will be safe.

Women who are nursing or pregnant should consult with their doctors before drinking kombucha. Because of the acidic and slightly alcoholic nature of kombucha, children younger than the age of six should not drink it. Children older than the age of six may drink kombucha in small volumes.

Please read instructions very carefully before starting a batch of kombucha. If you purchased your SCOBY online, the supplier likely included a list of instructions in the package. Chances are you can trust those instructions, but to double-check, be sure to read my instructions, too.

Kombucha should never smell or taste foul. It should taste slightly sweet yet vinegary and should smell this way, too. Home-brewed kombucha tends to be much stronger than store-bought kombucha, so the scent and taste will be much more pungent than store-bought kombucha. This is normal. If there is ever a putrid smell or the flavor does not sit right in your mouth, throw out the whole batch and start fresh with a new SCOBY.

Homemade kombucha can get so strong that drinking it is very similar to drinking vinegar. The optimal pH of kombucha should be on the acidic end, between 2.5 and 4.5. An acidic pH prohibits kombucha from becoming contaminated with bad bacteria. A pH lower than 2.5 is too acidic for human consumption and will need to be diluted before drinking. If the pH of your kombucha is ever below 2.5, add more tea and sugar and check the PH again before bottling it. A pH higher than 4.5 will create an environment that is optimal for bad bacteria to grow.

While it is perfectly fine to drink kombucha every day, most people caution against drinking more than 6 to 8 ounces of home-brewed kombucha each day. Commercially made kombucha is subject to many controls and tests, which makes it safe for drinking a larger amount. Since most people who brew kombucha (including myself) do not own advanced pH- and bacteria-testing equipment, it is wise to drink a lesser amount rather than risk upsetting the balance in your digestive system.

If you are concerned about sustaining a certain pH level in your kombucha, you can buy pH test strips to get a general idea of the how strong the kombucha is. For a more exact pH reading, you would need to buy a pH tester, as the pH test strips can give ambiguous readings. It is not necessary to test the pH of every kombucha batch, but I do recommend testing it periodically, especially when you think your kombucha is becoming too strong.

Should you brew a batch of bad kombucha and experience negative side effects, consult a doctor immediately. When in doubt, always, ALWAYS throw it out and start over. Provided the SCOBY you use to start your first batch of kombucha is healthy and provided you follow the instructions, it is unlikely a bad batch will result. Still, bad kombucha can cause harmful side effects, so play it safe.

Have fun with your home-brewed kombucha!

The active probiotics and yeasts in kombucha feed off of tea and sugar.

# Basic Kombucha:

## Ingredients (yields just under 1 gallon of kombucha):

- 1 kombucha SCOBY
- 1 (scant) gallon spring water or well water. Don't use water from your faucet because it probably has chlorine and/or fluoride in it.
- 10 black tea or green tea (no frills) tea bags*
- 1 cup cane sugar

*Be sure to use tea that is either 100 percent black or 100 percent green. Many companies add orange peel to black tea, which has essential oils in it that are not good for brewing. Stick to the 100 percent pure teas for the best results.

## You Will Also Need:

- Large pot for boiling water
- Large (1 gallon or more) glass jug/container for fermenting the kombucha
- Long-handled spoon for stirring
- Stick-on or floating thermometer
- Cheesecloth or breathable dish towel
- Stretchy rubber band
- A glass pitcher or other efficient method of transferring the kombucha from the jug to bottles or the dispenser you will be using to drink the kombucha out of
- Small fine strainer (we use a metal coffee strainer)
- Glass bottles with sealable lids. Both screw-top and flip-cap bottles work, and dark glass works best because kombucha does not like sunlight.

Add water to a sanitized pot before boiling

Covering your jug with cheesecloth allows the kombucha to breathe as it brews.

## Optional Tools:

- Distilled white vinegar for cleaning your kombucha jug

- Heating device such as an electric heating pad. These work great for helping to maintain the temperature of your kombucha if your house is cold during the winter.

- Space blanket. May be used to trap in heat. During cold spells, wrapping the kombucha jug with a heating pad and securing it with a space blanket works wonders.

# How to make homemade kombucha:

1. Sanitize everything you are using to make kombucha. You can do this by running it through the dishwasher, hand-washing in very hot water with soap, or by coating it in distilled white vinegar.

2. Boil water. If you are making 1 gallon of kombucha, you do not need to boil the entire 1 gallon—just enough (½ gallon or so) to brew the tea. This way you can add the remaining water to cool the tea once it's brewed.

3. Once water has reached a boiling point, remove it from heat and add tea bags. Steep the tea for 8 to 10 minutes and then remove the bags.

4. Add the cane sugar and stir well to dissolve.

5. Allow the tea to cool to roughly 75° to 85° (or if you only boiled half a gallon of water, add the remaining half gallon of cool water so that the hot water cools faster).

6. Once the tea is in the optimal temperature range, add the SCOBY (if this is your first time making kombucha and you bought your SCOBY online, simply remove it from its package and slip it in).

7. If you have a sticky thermometer that can be stuck to a surface, stick it on the outside of the jug (optional).

8. Cover the jug with cheesecloth so that the kombucha can continually breathe.

9. Secure the cheesecloth with a stretchy rubber band.

10. Place jug in a dark place (closet) that stays relatively warm and is not disturbed by people and light.

11. Allow kombucha to brew for five to seven days (the longer it brews, the more sugar it eats and the stronger it is).

12. Continually check the temperature of the kombucha. For best results, it should stay in the 70° to 85° range. If it falls below 70°, it's not a huge deal, it will just take longer for the kombucha to brew. If the kombucha gets above 85°, the probiotics may die. If you see any mold (it will look like bread mold . . . green/white and fuzzy circles), discard the SCOBY and the whole batch of kombucha.

13. When your kombucha is ready, remove the cheesecloth. NOTE: You will notice your SCOBY is bigger—it will grow to the width of the container it's in and a second SCOBY will form. SCOBYs will always continue to grow. Once a SCOBY gets to be a couple of inches thick, I recommend peeling

a layer or two off and either discard it or give it to a friend along with some starter liquid so that they can brew their own kombucha.

14. Now that your kombucha has completed the first fermentation, you can either bottle it and be finished or add ingredients by following the recipes in this book. I find it is easiest to pour the kombucha liquid out of the jug and into a smaller pitcher. Using the pitcher, it is easy to pour the kombucha into bottles.

15. Once you have bottled the kombucha, you can either take a break, leave your SCOBY and starter liquid in the jug covered with cheesecloth bound with a rubber band, or you can brew a new batch. As long as SCOBYs are in a healthy environment, they can sit for months at a time between batches. When taking a break, simply leave the jug in a warm, dark place that doesn't get disturbed often (just as you would if you were brewing a batch) and be sure to inspect the SCOBY before brewing a new batch, especially if it has been sitting for more than a couple weeks. For every one inch of SCOBY, I typically save about two inches worth of starter liquid.

16. If you choose to add ingredients for a secondary fermentation, follow the recipe instructions and leave the bottles of flavored komucha at room temperature in a dark place for two to three days. During this process, the bacteria and yeast cultures eat the sugar you added (fructose from the juice or cane sugar) and continue to ferment. This makes the kombucha

a little stronger and fizzy ("effervescent" is what the industry calls it). It is important to note that a small SCOBY will form in each bottle during the secondary fermentation, which can be strained out before drinking.

17. Place kombucha in the refrigerator for twenty-four hours before consuming for the best results. The cooler temperature will slow the fermentation (although the kombucha will continue to ferment), and refrigerating it seems to help in achieving a bubbly drink.

18. Get creative with your flavors, pat yourself on the back, and enjoy your homebrewed kombucha!

# Pomegranate Kombucha (Kombucha and Juice)

I flavored the first few batches of kombucha I brewed using various 100 percent fruit juices, such as pomegranate, pear, blueberry, and cranberry. This is a very quick and easy way to add flavor as well as vitamins, minerals, and antioxidants to the kombucha.

Generally, 1 cup of juice per 1 gallon (or ¾ gallon) of kombucha is sufficient to put the kombucha through secondary fermentation. Pomegranate juice adds sweet, tart flavor as well as antioxidants.

## Ingredients (yields just under 1 gallon of kombucha):
- **1 cup 100 percent pomegranate juice (or juice of choice)**
- **¾ gallon kombucha (page 251)**

## Instructions

1. In a large pitcher or jug, combine the juice and the kombucha and stir well.

2. Pour the pomegranate kombucha into sealable bottles and leave them in a warm, dark place for two to three days for secondary fermentation.

3. Refrigerate the kombucha to slow the secondary fermentation.

*Note:*

*When adding juice to kombucha for a secondary fermentation, the result does not come out as fizzy as if you added fresh fruit including the fruit pulp. Kombucha reacts more strongly during secondary fermentation when ingredients that have texture are added, resulting in a much fizzier beverage. Nevertheless, adding juice is tasty, healthful, and easy!*

# Lemon Ginger Kombucha

Lemon ginger kombucha is very handy to have on hand during cold and flu season! Not only does kombucha help boost the immune system, but both lemon and ginger are also great for fighting colds. Plus the beverage tastes great! When combined, lemon and ginger yields an almost creamy flavor, soothing the bite you'd expect from the ingredients on their own and leaving your palate happy!

## Ingredients:
- 4 cups water
- 3 tbsps fresh ginger, grated
- 3 tbsps fresh lemon juice
- ½ cup cane sugar
- ¾ gallon kombucha (page 251)

## Instructions:

1. Add the water and grated ginger to a pot and bring to a full boil. Reduce the temperature to medium and keep the water bubbling for about 5 minutes to infuse the water with ginger flavor.

2. Remove pot from heat and add the lemon juice and sugar, stirring to dissolve the sugar.

3. Allow the pot to sit until it cools to room temperature. This will allow the ginger to infuse the tea with flavor.

4. Once ginger tea is cool, add it to a pitcher or jug and combine it with the kombucha (depending on the size of your pitcher, you may need to do this in halves).

5. Stir kombucha and ginger tea together and then pour it into glass bottles. Try to get as much of the ginger in the bottles with the kombucha as possible. Secure with a tight cap.

6. Leave bottles in a warm, dark place for two to four days to allow it to undergo secondary fermentation. Refrigerate kombucha once the second ferment is complete to slow the fermentation.

7. When you're ready to drink the kombucha, strain it into a glass using a fine strainer to get the ginger pulp and newly grown SCOBY out. Discard the pulp and enjoy your healthy beverage!

# Apple Cinnamon Kombucha

Apple cinnamon is my favorite kombucha flavor during the fall and winter months. The warm spices and sweet, tart apple make for a cozy beverage. Because the ingredients in this beverage are uncomplicated and easy to find any time of year at any grocery store, this is a great recipe to make in a large batch to store in bottles and enjoy for weeks.

## Ingredients:
- 4 apple-flavored tea bags
- 4 cups water
- 1 tsp ground cinnamon
- ⅛ tsp ground nutmeg
- ½ cup sugar
- 3 ounces dried apple rings (no preservatives)*
- ¾ gallon kombucha (page 251)

*Purchase your dried apples from a natural food store to get them without preservatives. The ingredients list should be simple for any dried fruit you add to kombucha and it is worth paying a little extra to be sure the kombucha stays healthy and doesn't have an adverse reaction with unnecessary chemicals or ingredients.

## Instructions:

1. In a saucepan, add 4 cups of water and bring it to a boil.

2. Remove water from heat, add the apple-flavored tea bags, and steep tea for 5 to 8 minutes.

3. Add the sugar and stir to dissolve.

4. Set the sweetened apple tea aside and allow it to cool to room temperature. You can speed up this process by putting it in the refrigerator or an ice bath until it reaches a lukewarm temperature.

5. Slice apple rings in half and put two slices (one ring) in each bottle before filling it with kombucha. Seal the bottles.

6. Leave bottles in a warm, dark place for two to four days to allow kombucha to go through secondary fermentation.

7. Refrigerate the kombucha. When ready to drink, use a strainer to strain out the small SCOBY that formed in the bottle during secondary fermentation.

# Blackberry Sage Kombucha

The tart and sweet blackberries give a great deal of life to the kombucha, as berries tend to make for a bubblier beverage and infuse very noticeable flavor. The sage gives the beverage a soft earthiness. Blackberries are rich in antioxidants and fiber. They aid in digestion, promote cardiovascular health, protect against cancer cells and neurological diseases, and more. Sage is an herb related to mint and is full of health benefits and medicinal uses. It is an anti-inflammatory, improves memory, can be used as an antiseptic, helps with allergic reactions and mosquito bites, and is packed with antioxidants!

## Ingredients:

- **2 cups ripe blackberries**
- **.65 ounces sage leaves, chopped (about 15 to 20 large sage leaves)**
- **1⁄3 cup cane sugar**
- **3⁄4 gallon kombucha (page 251)**

## Instructions:

1. Heat blackberries in a saucepan, covered, over medium heat. As the blackberries heat up and begin to bubble and soften, mash them with a fork.

2. Once a pulpy juice forms add the sugar and sage and bring to a gentle boil.

3. Reduce heat to medium-low, cover the saucepan, and allow the flavors to cook together, about 15 to 20 minutes. Do not allow mixture to boil or cook for too long, or else it will become very thick.

4. Leave bottles in a warm, dark place for two to four days to allow kombucha to go through secondary fermentation.

5. In a large pot or pitcher, combine the kombucha and blackberry sage mixture. Mix together well and then pour the blackberry sage kombucha into sealable bottles, including the sage leaves and blackberry pulp. Seal the bottles.

6. Allow the kombucha to go through its secondary fermentation by allowing it to sit in a warm, dark place for two to three days. Note that the longer the kombucha sits, the more sugar will be eaten by the probiotics, which will result in a less sweet and more fizzy beverage.

7. Refrigerate for twenty-four hours after the secondary fermentation is complete. This slows the secondary fermentation, but the kombucha will continue to ferment and get fizzier the longer it sits in the refrigerator.

8. When you're ready to drink the kombucha, use a small fine strainer to strain out the sage leaves, blackberry pulp, and whatever small SCOBY has formed during the secondary fermentation. Discard all the pulp and enjoy the beverage!

# Jasmine Kombucha

Although kombucha prefers 100 percent black tea for brewing, you can add other flavored teas can be added for secondary fermentation. Consider using your favorite tea flavors and even use loose tea.

This relaxing beverage smells and tastes wonderful. Jasmine makes a naturally soothing tea that is known for calming the mood and lowering heart rate. Studies show jasmine can prevent stroke and esophageal cancer. Jasmine tea adds a soft, floral flavor and is an easy way of flavoring kombucha for secondary fermentation.

## Ingredients:
- 3 cups water
- 3 jasmine tea bags
- ½ cup sugar
- ¾ gallon kombucha (page 251)

## Instructions:

1. In a saucepan, bring the water to a boil.

2. Add the tea bags and steep for 5 to 8 minutes.

3. Add the sugar and stir to dissolve.

4. Allow jasmine tea to cool to room temperature. To speed up this process, you can put the pot of tea in an ice bath or pour the tea in a jug and put it in the refrigerator until it reaches a lukewarm temperature.

5. In a large pitcher or jug, combine the jasmine tea with the kombucha and stir.

6. Pour jasmine kombucha into sealable bottles and then seal them shut.

7. Leave them in a warm, dark place for two to four days to allow for secondary fermentation.

8. Refrigerate the bottles after secondary fermentation. When ready to drink, open bottles carefully in case pressure built during secondary fermentation.

# Pineapple Kombucha

Are you looking for that kombucha that is ultra fizzy and sweet? Well here it is! When pineapple chunks are added to kombucha for secondary fermentation, a very fizzy beverage results. I have found that the more acidic fruits yield the more effervescent probiotic beverages. For this reason, acidic fruits are great for flavoring these beverages, but it is important to use non-breakable bottles and to be very careful when opening the bottles after secondary fermentation.

Screw-top bottles are recommended for bottling this particular recipe, as the pressure that builds during secondary fermentation from the pineapple becomes so great that the beverage overflows when it is opened out of a flip-cap bottle. With screw tops, a minimal amount of air is always allowed out and you are able to slowly twist the cap to relieve pressure before opening. For safety purposes, do not hand children bottles of pineapple kombucha, as they may explode all over and can be unsafe for them to open. It is best to always look away from the bottle while carefully opening it and never point it at anyone. The same is true for any fizzy probiotic beverage in this book.

While pineapple kombucha requires a little additional forethought and precaution, it has an incredible tropical flavor and is so refreshing in the spring and early summertime when pineapples are in season!

## Ingredients:
- 2 cups fresh pineapple, chopped into ¼" to ½" pieces
- ¾ gallon of homemade kombucha (page 251)

## Instructions:

1. Evenly distribute the chopped pineapple between the bottles you're using for bottling.

2. Pour the kombucha into the bottles with the pineapple.

3. Seal the bottles and place them in a dark, warm spot, such as a cabinet or closet.

4. Allow bottles to sit for two to three days in a warm, dark place so that the kombucha goes through a secondary fermentation.

5. Refrigerate the kombucha for at least twenty-four hours before consuming. Allowing the kombucha to refrigerate for longer than a day will result in more effervescent kombucha.

# Raspberry Mint Kombucha

The combination of raspberries and mint make a sweet, slightly tart, and refreshing beverage with an abundance of flavor. Fresh raspberries are heated with mint leaves to allow all the flavors to open up and infuse. Raspberry mint kombucha is a fun beverage any time of year, and is particularly great in the summer when raspberries are in season.

**Ingredients:**
- **6 ounces fresh raspberries**
- **.75 ounces fresh mint leaves, roughly chopped**
- **½ cup sugar**
- **¼ cup water**
- **¾ gallon kombucha (page 251)**

## Instructions:

1. Remove mint leaves from the stems and using your fingers, rip them into smaller pieces (in half or thirds is fine).

2. Place raspberries, mint leaves, sugar, and water into a small saucepan and heat over medium. Bring mixture to a full boil.

3. Using a fork, smash the raspberries until they lose form.

4. Reduce heat to medium-low and allow the mixture to continue to boil gently for about 5 minutes to allow the mint to infuse.

5. Remove from heat and allow mixture to cool to room temperature. To speed up this process, pour it into a bowl or glass and place in the refrigerator.

6. In a large pitcher or jug, combine the kombucha and raspberry-mint mixture.

7. Stir to combine, then pour the kombucha into bottles.

8. Once you reach the bottom, spoon the raspberry and mint pulp into the bottles, trying to distribute the pulp evenly among the bottles.

9. Leave the bottles in a dark, warm place for two to four days to allow the kombucha to go through secondary fermentation.

10. Refrigerate at least twenty-four hours before drinking. The kombucha will get fizzier the longer you wait to drink it.

11. When you're ready to drink the kombucha, use a fine strainer to strain out the newly formed SCOBY and the raspberry and mint pulp. Enjoy!

# Fig Kombucha

Incorporating figs into kombucha, smoothies, or even baked goods is an excellent way of achieving a naturally sweet treat. Figs are high in fructose and have a subtle flavor, making them a wonderful way to add sweetness without overpowering flavor. This is a fizzy and sweet kombucha with nothing but "original" flavor. Using 1 fig per 16-ounce bottle, you can scale this recipe to any size you would like. If you use the full ¾ gallon, you will end up with 6 bottles.

## Ingredients (yields just under 1 gallon of kombucha):
- 6 ripe figs, chopped into small bits
- ¾ gallon kombucha (page 251)

## Instructions:

1. Add 1 finely chopped fig to each 16-ounce bottle.

2. Seal bottles and leave them in a warm dark place for two days for secondary fermentation.

3. Refrigerate fig kombucha for a full twenty-four hours for best result before consuming.

4. When ready to consume, strain the fig pulp (and the newly-formed SCOBY) using a fine strainer and enjoy!

# Other Probiotic Drinks

## More on Making Kombucha and Water Kefir (Tibicos)

Water kefir grains (tibicos) are merely kefir grains that have been developed to culture nondairy beverages. Rather than appearing white or creamy, tibicos are translucent. You can use them to culture sugar water, coconut water, or fruit juice into water kefir, coconut kefir, or cider. As far as their history and properties, they are identical to the kefir grains covered earlier. I include them here with kombucha, because they can be used in much the same way. However, tibicos can culture a drink in as quickly as 1–2 days, while the kombucha culture takes as long as 7–14 days.

Kombucha probably originated in Northeast Asia, specifically in the Manchurian region of China, but possibly in Japan. The first mention of kombucha appeared in Manchuria around 330 BC, while another story places it in Japan in 415 AD. However, because a seaweed tea in the region also carried a similar name, no one is sure that this referred to the fermented tea drink. Centuries later, kombucha emerged in a historical record in Russia, which may have been its actual place of birth.

The kombucha mother is a unique culture. First of all, it is the most visible of all SCOBYs, looking like a chunk of rubber or silicon. In addition, while kefir and ginger beer cultures mostly drop to the bottom of any liquid (at least until it gets carbonated), the much bulkier kombucha SCOBY floats on top of the drink. It can cover the entire surface area of the container and grow to an inch or more in thickness. The species of bacteria most responsible for the physical appearance of the kombucha mother is *Bacillus coagulans* (also known as *Lactobacillus sporogenes*). The porous, rubbery mat it creates provides a great living environment for up to a dozen additional kinds of yeasts and bacteria.

You can either obtain a kombucha SCOBY from someone who has some extra culture to share, order one online, or grow one yourself from a bottle of kombucha. Growing your own is fairly easy. Start with a store-bought bottle of kombucha, pouring this into a larger jar or plastic container along with some tea and sugar. After a few days, you will see a white film growing near the top of the liquid, which at first you might mistake for mold. Each day you check it, you will notice that the film has grown thicker, eventually becoming a deep mat that covers the top of your fermenting drink.

This flat blob is your very own kombucha mushroom, which you can use to ferment your own probiotic drinks and foods. Anytime you want to culture something new, you can gently move the mushroom to a new container. If it gets too big, you can cut it and divide the pieces. You can use your extra culture to ferment another drink, share it with a friend, or compost it. Used SCOBYs are great for your garden also, where beneficial microorganisms contribute to healthy soil, helping plants grow and stay healthy.

# How to Make Water Kefir (Using Tibicos)

Water kefir is made by using tibicos (water kefir grains) to ferment sugar water. Most people use brown sugar, cane sugar, or maple syrup, or another wholesome sweetener that provides more minerals than the depleted white sugar sold in stores. When the cultures do not have enough minerals available, they will not ferment effectively. Usually, water kefir grains (tibicos) are used to make water kefir, though milk kefir grains will work also.

Adding some sea salt (anywhere from a pinch to a teaspoon, depending on your preference) also can help ensure that minerals are present. Another option is to add some cut fruit or ginger to the ferment. This will supply a few more minerals as well as some flavor. But bear in mind that you will need to pick out the kefir grains later on from the fruit or ginger. And it is always possible to add flavor after the fermentation, once these grains are removed.

As an alternative to sugar water, you can use coconut water from a young coconut, which contains enough sugar and minerals that it does not need any added sweeteners or minerals. Young coconuts and coconut water are increasingly popular. You can find both at many health food stores as well as Latin American and Asian food markets.

# Water Kefir (or Coconut Water Kefir)

Makes 1 quart

## Required materials:

- 1 large mixing bowl (glass, plastic, or wood, but not metal)

- 2 glass jars (quart-sized mason jars are good)

- 1 silicon spatula or wooden spoon

- 1 plastic strainer

- Cheesecloth, towel, or a sprouting lid for the jar

## Ingredients:

- 1 quart of filtered (nonchlorinated) water or young coconut water

- ¼ cup (4 tbsps) of water kefir grains (tibicos)

- Sweetener (not needed if using coconut water): ¼ cup of cane sugar, brown sugar, or maple syrup

- Optional: Chopped or sliced fruit of your choice or sliced ginger root

- Optional: Dash of sea salt

## Process:

- Wash all equipment thoroughly before using.

- Place kefir grains in the jar, fill it with water, and gently stir in the sweetener.

- Optional: Throw in a dash of sea salt, which adds trace minerals to support the fermentation.

- Put the jar in an undisturbed place away from direct sunlight. Cover it loosely with the cheesecloth, towel, or a sprouting lid (which provides air circulation).

- Check your water kefir after 12 hours and again after 24 hours. Swish it around a little bit in the jar and then taste it with a clean spoon. If it's not sour enough for you yet, then give it another 12 hours. The fermentation will be faster in warm weather and slower when the air is cool. If you want to slow it down and fine tune your kefir, then you can put the whole jar in the refrigerator, where it will continue to ferment more slowly.

- Once you are ready to stop the fermentation, use the strainer over a bowl to strain out the kefir grains from the beverage. If you have also used fruit or ginger, you must pick out the kefir grains from these; my favorite tool for this is wooden/bamboo chopsticks. Your kefir can be enjoyed immediately or stored in a jar or plastic container in the refrigerator.

- Reuse your kefir grains immediately in a new batch of sugar water or else store them for up to two weeks in the refrigerator (sitting in some sugar water).

## Checking for Proper Fermentation

Your nose and the little bubbles should tell you if your kombucha is fermenting properly. But if you suspect something has gone wrong and the culture has failed, then you need to check it more closely. The best method of investigation is to use pH test strips. If, after 3–4 days of fermentation, the pH of your fluid is not in the 2.5–3.0 range, then it is not acidic enough and something has gone wrong. Dump it out, sterilize everything, and start again with a new culture. Also, if there is a strong kerosene smell coming from the kombucha, as opposed to a yeast or vinegar smell, that means something else has gotten in there and you need to dump it.

## Fizzy Kombucha

If your kombucha is not as effervescent as you would like, you can conduct a secondary fermentation in a bottle. To fuel this second stage, you can use juice (which provides a nice flavor), or else use some more sweet tea. Either way, you will end up with a kombucha soda. Take a plastic bottle with a tight-fitting lid, such as a soda or water bottle. (You can use a glass jar or bottle also, but it is easiest to check the air pressure in a plastic vessel.) Fill it three-quarters of the way with your fermented kombucha and top this off with some additional juice. Tighten the lid and leave this at room temperature to continue fermenting. It probably will be ready in 2–7 days, but check it every day or so.

If you used a plastic bottle, then checking it is as simple as squeezing the sides of the bottle. If it has really puffed out so that squeezing is difficult, your drink should be ready. Open with caution, since the contents may be under pressure. Unless you've shaken the bottle, it really should not explode on you, but there will be a release of air pressure as there is when opening any soda bottle. Taste and decide if it's fizzy enough for you. If not, tighten the lid and give it another 12 hours or so.

## Storing and Reusing Your Kombucha SCOBY

Storing a kombucha SCOBY is easier than storing kefir grains, simply because it takes longer to ferment a batch. This means that you can start fermenting some sweet tea with a kombucha SCOBY and just leave it for as long as a couple of weeks. The fermented liquid may be too acidic to drink, but your culture should still be alive after that time and you can begin using it again. While you can store your SCOBY in the refrigerator, this can cause the yeasts to go dormant, so the above method is better.

## Rejuvelac

Rejuvelac is a fermented beverage made from sprouted cereal grains, such as wheat, barley, rye, oats, triticale, millet, amaranth, quinoa, brown rice, wild rice, or buckwheat. People have been making fermented drinks with grains for thousands of years, but the raw food advocate Ann Wigmore is credited with popularizing rejuvelac as part of a holistic health diet. It's pretty sour and definitely qualifies as an acquired taste unless you add some sugar, honey, or other sweetener. Alternatively, this makes a great base ingredient for sodas, or you can mix it with juice, and it can be used to culture anything else in this book.

- ½ cup organic grains such as wheat, rye, barley, or oats (whole-seeded, not ground or cracked)

- Water

- Optional: 1 tbsp yogurt whey or water kefir

Rinse the grains. Put them in the jar or container and cover them with water. Let them soak overnight. In the morning, drain the water from the grains, rinse them, and put them back in the jar. The rinsing prevents mold. Continue to rinse twice per day for 1–2 days, until grains form small white tails, indicating that they have sprouted. Rinse them once more and put grains in the large container. You could use the same jar if it's big enough (be sure to rinse before reusing). Cover the grains with one quart of water. Add yogurt whey or other culture, if you choose to use this (if not, the natural yeasts and bacteria on grains will ferment the water). Cover the container loosely, checking it by tasting every 24 hours. This fermentation normally takes 1–3 days, and the later you let it go, the more sour it will be. Then pour out the liquid, which is the consumable part. The grains have left the better part of their nutrition in the liquid and are spent, so you can compost them. Feel free to add some sweetener or combine the rejuvelac with juice to make it drinkable.

This section is reserved for three special drinks. They could be considered sodas or smoothies, but all three are made a bit differently from the other drinks.

## Probiotic Lemonade

Makes about 2 quarts

This only takes a few more minutes than dissolving one of those chemical-filled lemonade envelopes in water. This drink is probiotic from the start by virtue of the cultured drink (kombucha, cider, etc.) you have added. But if you can wait for a richer ferment, prepare the drink in advance and let all the ingredients stand together for 24–48 hours. Also, see the separate Lemon-Lime Soda recipe, which is similar. Try this lemonade on your kids!

- Juice of 5 lemons
- ½ cup kombucha, cider, water kefir, or yogurt whey
- 1½–2 quarts water
- ¼–½ cup sugar or honey

Mix together all ingredients and let the drink sit in a jar or container for 24–48 hours or until it reaches desired sourness. If it's too sour, feel free to thin it out with more water or add extra honey or sugar. Garnish with a sprig of mint or slices of lemon.

# Watermelon Kombucha Cooler

Makes about 2 cups

- 1 cup ripe watermelon
- 1½ cups kombucha or water kefir
- Honey or sugar, to taste

Blend watermelon to purée it. If chunks remain, strain them out. For a frozen drink, freeze watermelon or purée first, then blend with kombucha or water kefir. If you do not freeze the purée, then you can stir it directly into the kombucha.

# Pineapple Tapache

Makes 3–4 quarts

This delicious beverage from Mexico may well be my favorite drink in this book. The recipe involves fermenting a whole pineapple (cut into chunks) in sweetened water with spices. You can culture it with water kefir grains (tibicos), yogurt whey, or cider. Otherwise, just let the naturally present bacteria culture it themselves. Traditionally, people cut up the peel and put this in to get plenty of bacteria. If you use the rind, then please cut off the bottom and discard this part, as ripe pineapples often have a little mold at the base of the core.

- 3–4 quarts water
- 1 fresh pineapple, peeled and cut into chunks
- 3 cups natural cane sugar or brown sugar
- 1 tsp vanilla extract
- 1 cinnamon stick or one tsp ground cinnamon
- Optional: 1 tbsp apple pie spice

Put the pineapple chunks in a very large container or jar, covering it with water. Use enough water to cover the pineapple—probably about half (2 quarts) of your water. Also add the sugar and spices. Then add your kefir/yogurt/cider culture, if you use any. Cover loosely and let it ferment. After 48 hours, add another quart of water and cover it loosely again. Let it sit for 12 hours this time before tasting. If it is sour enough for you, then drink some and refrigerate the rest. If it needs more time, add more water and give it an additional 12 hours to ferment. It should be ready at that point, and if it is too sour, you can add a little sugar, honey, or apple juice. You can eat the pineapple chunks or compost them. I feed some to my backyard chickens (the subject of another book) who love pineapple. They need their probiotics, too!

# Healthy Energy Drinks

Now, let's cover energy drinks. In theory, these are a great idea, but in practice, most commercially produced energy drinks do not provide healthy results. They are designed to give you a short-term fix with massive quantities of caffeine and sugar, combined with a questionable cocktail of herbs, vitamins, and amino acids such as guanine and taurine. Guanine is a stimulant derived from the guarana plant, which is high in caffeine, while the amino acid taurine serves to concentrate caffeine in the body.

Energy drinks have been blamed, rightly or wrongly, for a number of deaths. Many experts consider them to be unhealthy and perhaps dangerous to consume, particularly in combination with other active substances such as alcohol, tobacco, and more caffeine. Instead of consuming substances that squeeze the body for a short-term energy rush, why not make your own probiotic energy drink using safe and wholesome foods? These drinks can nourish the body and boost energy levels naturally. You can find many of the ingredients you need in your kitchen or cupboard.

Start with a base of kefir, water kefir, rejuvelac, or kombucha. Then add any of the ingredients below, each of which has been proven to have a positive effect on a person's energy. As always, if you are suffering from a particular medical condition, consult a qualified physician or natural health expert before making your own energy drinks or consuming any of the following substances that your body may not have encountered before (such as ginseng).

**Cinnamon and Honey:** Cinnamon has a warming flavor that adds a special touch to many foods and drinks. Honey, especially raw and unpasteurized honey with its enzymes intact, delivers a simple carbohydrate boost to your body. In a recent study, researchers found that cinnamon enhanced participants' brain functions and cognitive processing. Participants who smelled cinnamon or chewed cinnamon gum achieved better scores on a computer test of several different cognitive and memory functions. Separate research showed that taking half a teaspoon of honey sprinkled with cinnamon, around 3:00 p.m. each day, increases the body's vitality within a week at this time of the day when many people's body clocks are on a low ebb. It seems that a sprinkle of cinnamon is all you need to add to a homemade energy drink to get these benefits (and even the smell alone might do the job!). Large quantities of cinnamon can be toxic.

**Citrus:** Have you ever drank a glass of orange juice and felt more alert? When I stopped drinking coffee regularly many years ago, I often drank orange juice in the morning, and I swore it helped me wake up. It turns out I was not imagining this. Research has shown that both the smell of citrus and the acidity of the juice can awaken your body. Plus, it provides a great flavoring for any kefir, kombucha, natural soda, or energy drink. Try squeezing a little orange, lemon, lime, mandarin, or grapefruit juice into your drink.

**Green Tea:** Green tea can help increase your energy levels in several ways. First, since it contains some caffeine, you get a short-term boost. Typically, green tea contains much less caffeine than a cup of coffee, an energy drink, or a caffeinated soda. If you want the other benefits of green tea without the caffeine, you can opt for naturally decaffeinated green tea. To put green tea's caffeine level in perspective, consider the following list of the typical quantities of caffeine in these common sources. I think you'll find that green tea contains a smaller amount of caffeine than most alternatives:

- Green tea (8 oz): 25–40 mg of caffeine

- Black tea (8 oz): 15–60 mg

- Coca-Cola® (8 oz): 20–30 mg

- Monster™/Red Bull™/Rockstar™ Energy Drinks (8.0–8.4 oz): 80–92 mg

- 5-Hour Energy™ (2 oz): 207 mg

- Dark Chocolate (1.5 oz): 26 mg

- Milk chocolate (1.5 oz): 9 mg

The second way that green tea boosts your energy level is with a natural substance it contains called L-theanine, which has been shown to increase alertness without the jitters of caffeine. And third, EGCG is a powerful antioxidant in green tea that scrubs your body of free radicals. This should help you feel more energetic over time.

**Ginseng:** Thousands of years' worth of testing on humans has demonstrated ginseng's near-magical properties to the people of China, Korea, Japan, and beyond. More recently, Western studies have verified that panax ginseng (the most effective kind) really does boost energy. It may reach this result by improving blood flow to the brain. This is a natural increase that can be sustainable; it has none of the ups and downs associated with caffeine. Ginseng also is revered in Asia for its effect on sexual potency, which may also be related to the improved blood flow to the brain. Studies have proven that people who take ginseng before a test have better memory recognition and higher scores.

There are several kinds of ginseng, including American and Siberian, but panax ginseng (also known as red ginseng, Chinese red ginseng, or Korean ginseng) is the one that works best. I've tried a lot of herbs that are said to be good for one thing or another. Not one of them has ever worked on me the way panax ginseng does. If your energy is at a low ebb or you are feeling like you are getting a cold, drinking a strong cup of red ginseng tea might give you new life. It lifts me up a couple of levels on the energy meter and puts me back in a place where I feel like my body has the strength to fight off a pesky cold. If I felt like taking a nap before consuming ginseng, I often feel like running a mile or two after taking it (not always right away but within a few hours).

As for its potency powers? I will let you try it and see for yourself. Of course, make sure your physician approves if you have a medical condition or are on any medication, especially since I view ginseng as the strongest energy supplement in this chapter.

Ginseng tea, extract, and powder generally are the best ways to add this to a probiotic beverage. It seems to deliver the most benefit at doses above 200 mg, but the label for the tea or extract you get may or may not include this information. Following the label directions is the best place to start, and from there you can adjust the amounts to your liking. If you cannot find ginseng locally at an Asian market or health food store, try conducting an online search for "red ginseng." It's worth every penny.

**Mint:** The smell and taste of mint can revive the senses. Try using a sprig of mint as an edible garnish or crush some mint and then soak it in water to make an extract for flavoring drinks. Another simple option is to brew some peppermint, spearmint, or pennyroyal tea, cool it, and add it to drinks.

## Putting It All Together

There is a recipe below for a homemade probiotic energy drink, which includes all of these suggested enhancers. You do not need to include all of them; just use the ones you like and have available. If you need a big boost, though, I would suggest trying the ginseng, as it often has a stronger effect on energy levels than any other food. From citrus to cinnamon to mint tea, you may already have some of the others in your kitchen or cupboard.

## Tea Bag Time Savers

If you do not have the time to brew up your own concoction, then here is a real time saver that just costs a few dollars. A number of tea companies, including Lipton®,

Celestial Seasonings™, and Bigelow®/AriZona Iced Tea®, make and sell tea bags that include several energy-enhancing ingredients. All are available at stores that sell herbal teas or online. Lipton makes lemon ginseng green tea, Celestial Seasonings makes honey lemon ginseng green tea, and Bigelow (branded as AriZona) makes green tea with ginseng and honey. Rather than chasing down all the ingredients and measuring them, you could spend a few dollars for a box of twenty-five tea bags. Each time you needed an energy drink, you could heat a half cup or so of water, brew the tea bag in it until it cools a bit, then top off the cup with water kefir, rejuvelac, or kombucha. Add a little more honey, cinnamon, mint, or citrus squeeze if you wish. Wow, that was easy!

Here are the recipes for green drinks (which come first) and the energy drink (at the end of this chapter).

# Secret Spinach Shake

Makes 4–6 cups

Sweet and dark fruit hide the two cups of baby spinach in this drink. You could use baby kale or other greens also. All fruit can be fresh or frozen.

- 1 ripe banana
- ½ cup orange juice
- 1 cup blueberries
- 1 cup pineapple
- 1 cup yogurt
- 2 cups baby spinach
- Honey or sugar, to taste

Place all ingredients in a blender. Blend, taste, adjust with additional honey or sugar, and serve.

# Green Chocolate Chia

Makes 2–3 cups

This recipe uses chia seeds, which are incredibly nutritious and available at health food stores. If you prefer, you could substitute poppy seeds, hemp seed hearts, flax seeds, or ground flaxseed meal . . . or leave out the seeds if you just want the green chocolate! If you use chia, then presoak it as follows: put the chia seeds in a small cup, cover it with a little of the liquid you will use in the recipe (such as kombucha or kefir), and let the seeds soak for 5 minutes. Pour this into your blender, scraping in as many of the sticky seeds as you can get. Feel free to use as much spirulina, green powder, or spinach as you can handle.

- 1 cup chocolate ice cream or frozen yogurt (or 1 cup yogurt + 1 packet cocoa mix)
- 1–3 tbsps chia seeds (presoaked as described above)
- 1–3 tbsps (or more) spirulina or green juice powder or 1 cup baby spinach greens
- ¼ tsp vanilla extract
- 1 cup kombucha, kefir, or rejuvelac
- Optional: Handful of fresh mint leaves
- Garnish with a sprig of fresh mint

Place all ingredients in a blender. Blend, taste, adjust with additional honey or sugar, and serve.

The Big Book of Juicing

# Kale, Banana, and Pear Smoothie

Makes 2–3 cups

This recipe combines some very healthy greens with an overpowering quantity of sweet, custardy fruit (bananas and pears). Kale is easy to grow in the home garden and it is quite cold-hardy; we are able to grow it almost year-round. If you can only find tougher, mature kale leaves, then tear off the leafy parts and omit the stems. Another idea is to run your kale through a juicer first and just add the juice to this smoothie. Or you can substitute baby spinach leaves.

- 2 bananas
- 1 cup milk or CRASH alternative
- 2 ripe pears, peeled and cut
- 2 cups baby kale or baby spinach
- ½ cup yogurt or cottage cheese

Place all ingredients in a blender. Blend, taste, adjust with additional honey or sugar, and serve.

# Beet and Green Kvass

Makes about 4–5 cups

Kvass is a traditional Russian drink, which usually is made with beets or dried rye bread. It is a sour-salty beverage. This recipe skips the rye bread, using only beets, greens, and celery. Due to these additional vegetables, it should be blended. You can culture this with yogurt whey, sauerkraut or natural pickle juice, or vegetable starter culture, or you can just skip the starter and rely on naturally present lactobacteria to ferment the vegetables a little more slowly (organic beets and celery have plenty of naturally present cultures). Like many fermented foods and drinks, kvass is an acquired taste. Those who do enjoy it often swear by its health benefits, some of them drinking kvass on a daily basis.

- 3 large beets, peeled and cut into cubes

- 1 quart water

- 1 stick celery, chopped

- Handful of baby spinach or baby kale

- 2 tsps whey/starter culture

- Optional: 1½–2 tsps sea salt

- Optional: 2 tbsps ginger (chopped) or 1 clove garlic (crushed)

Place all ingredients in a blender, blend them together, and then move the drink to a container or jar. Cover it loosely and allow your beverage to ferment at room temperature for 3–5 days. Before drinking, add a little salt or sugar if you wish.

# Savory Veggie Smoothie

This could be called V7, V9, or however many veggies you end up adding, though I don't wish to confuse it with a particular canned vegetable juice. You can make this as salty or spicy as you want by adding salt and jalapeno pepper. For an extra probiotic kick, throw in a little sauerkraut or natural pickles if you have some! If this smoothie is too fibrous for you, then another option is to run these veggies through a juicer and just add their juice to the blender along with the other ingredients.

- 1 cup tomato juice
- ½ cup carrot juice
- ½ cup kombucha, water kefir, or rejuvelac
- ½ cucumber, peeled
- 1 small celery stalk
- ¼ cup bell pepper
- ½ cup baby spinach or baby kale greens
- 1 small clove of garlic (crushed) or small handful of fresh chives
- 1 tsp lemon or lime juice
- Salt, black pepper, and cayenne pepper, to taste
- Optional: ½ jalapeno pepper
- Optional: ¼ cup sauerkraut or natural pickles

Place all ingredients in a blender. Blend, taste, adjust with additional honey or sugar, and serve.

# Carrot Seaweed Green Smoothie

Makes about 2 cups

You can buy dried seaweed in Asian and health food stores. Look for kelp (kombu), though most other kinds will work fine. Try incorporating a few different kinds of seaweed to create a diverse range of nutrition and taste. To rehydrate the seaweed, soak it in water for at least 2 hours or until it is soft. The seaweed will still be firm, but moist throughout.

- ½ cup dried seaweed (soaked in water for at least 2 hours or until tender)
- 1–1½ cups carrot juice
- ½ cup kombucha, water kefir, or rejuvelac
- ¼ inch fresh ginger, peeled and chopped
- Optional: 1 banana, if you want to go the sweeter route

# Healthy Energy Drink

Makes about 2 cups

- 1 cup water, boiled
- 200 milligrams panax ginseng (extract or powder) *or* 1 panax ginseng tea bag (100–500 milligram strength)
- 1 tsp dried green tea leaves *or* 1 green tea bag
- Squeeze of lemon, lime, grapefruit, or orange
- 1 cup kombucha, water kefir, or cider
- Honey or sugar, to taste

Pour water (slightly below boiling temperature) over ginseng and green tea. Let steep for 3 minutes. Remove tea bags or pour tea liquid into another cup or container, straining out the tea leaves if needed. Then let the tea sit or place in the refrigerator until it cools to below 100°F. Mix in honey or sugar if you wish. Then combine with other ingredients. Garnish with a sprig of mint or a slice of citrus.

# Grapefruit Mint Energy Drink

Makes 2–3 cups

- 2 cups kombucha or water kefir
- Juice of 1 grapefruit
- ¼ cup Mint Soda Syrup

Combine all ingredients and serve. Garnish with fresh mint.

## Mandarin Orange Spice Energy Drink

- 2 cups natural cider

- Juice of 3–4 mandarin oranges or tangerines

- Pinch of cinnamon

- Thin slice of ginger (peeled) *or* pinch of powdered ginger

- Optional: Pinch of allspice or 1 clove

Combine orange juice with spices. If you have time, put this in the refrigerator and let it sit for a few minutes or hours. Then combine with cider.

# Recipe Index